S0-BCZ-912

Mame Warren and Marion E. Warren

TIME

BALTIMORE AND LONDON

Maryland

EXPOSURES

1840 - 1940

THE JOHNS HOPKINS UNIVERSITY PRESS

A ROBERT G. MERRICK EDITION

THE JOHNS HOPKINS UNIVERSITY PRESS, Baltimore, Maryland 21218

THE JOHNS HOPKINS PRESS LTD, London

The paper in this book is acid-free and meets the guidelines for perma-
nence and durability of the Committee on Production Guidelines for
Book Longevity of the Council on Library Resources.

LIBRARY OF CONGRESS CATALOGING IN PUBLICATION DATA

Warren, Mame, 1950–
    Maryland time exposures, 1840–1940.

    1. Maryland—History—Pictorial works. 2. Maryland—Description
and travel—Views. I. Warren, Marion E. II. Title.
F181.W37 1984   975.2   84-47939
ISBN 0-8018-2496-6

This project was made possible in part by funds from the Maryland Humanities Council through a grant from the National
Endowment for the Humanities.

Generous support for this project was contributed by:

    MR. ROBERT G. MERRICK
    THE MARYLAND HERITAGE COMMITTEE
    THE MARYLAND HUMANITIES COUNCIL
    THE CHESAPEAKE & POTOMAC TELEPHONE COMPANY
    MARTIN MARIETTA CORPORATION
    MRS. CARLTON MITCHELL
    BALTIMORE GAS & ELECTRIC COMPANY
    BALTIMORE FEDERAL FINANCIAL FSA

The excerpt from Russell Baker's *Growing Up* (Congdon & Weed,
1982) is reprinted by permission of the author.

FRONTISPIECE PHOTOGRAPHS:

*Sailing on the Chesapeake Bay and its many tributaries is one of Mary-
land's greatest pleasures. These yachts were racing c. 1940 on the
Tred Avon River near Oxford on the Eastern Shore.*

*Friendly small towns like Mount Airy are everywhere in Maryland, but
the traveler comes upon them more frequently in the central section of
the state where the population is more concentrated.*

*The one quality that each of Maryland's southern counties has in
common with its neighbors is the fact that tobacco is still plentifully
cultivated.*

*Grant Wood could not have painted a more classic American farm
scene than this view in Western Maryland by Boonsboro photographer
C. D. Young—complete with Gothic-style barn.*

Contents

Preface

A fitting subtitle for this volume might be *A Sentimental Journey*. Over the last two years much ground has been covered: we traveled to every county in Maryland, often retracing our steps, since we have rambled this state many times in years gone by. Predictably, we found much that was familiar. We also observed many unexpected qualities in the history of the region we thought we knew so well. We hope that our readers will share our pleasure and discover new aspects of Maryland—both past and present.

Our intention is to engender an understanding and appreciation of Maryland's diversity. While a few characteristics are common to the entire state, many areas have features that are virtually unknown in some of the other counties. Oyster dredging, for example, is a prevalent occupation in many communities on the Eastern Shore—but an impossible career for someone living in Garrett County.

To vividly demonstrate the changing landscape, interests, and lifestyles in the state, we have organized the book geographically. First, we have divided it into four easily defined regions: the Eastern Shore, Central Maryland, Southern Maryland, and Western Maryland. Then, within each section we have arranged the pictures by location, just as one might encounter each scene if it were possible to wander the roads we know today while simultaneously moving about randomly in time between the years 1840 and 1940.

Thus we begin to see patterns: boatyards and steamboat landings line the Chesapeake Bay and its tributaries; farms are cultivated in every county; cities and towns offer greater commercial opportunities but lack some of the gentle tranquility of small towns and villages; railroads are everywhere and provide many services. We come upon the Chesapeake & Ohio Canal numerous times as we meander through Central and Western Maryland—just as we would on a weekend jaunt in a touring car c. 1920.

The time factor can occasionally be disconcerting. A Civil War view appears on the same page with a steam roller as pavement is laid for suburban expansion. The turn of one page takes us from an 1856 tintype to a parade celebrating the election of Woodrow Wilson. Yet it is these very juxtapositions which, taken as a whole, provide fascinating insights into a century of Maryland history.

Thousands of photographs were reviewed for this project. More than two thousand were actually copied and considered for inclusion in this book. Regrettably, it was possible to select fewer than six hundred. The remaining images, each an important historical document, as well as most of the photographs reproduced on these pages, have been cataloged in *The Robert G. Merrick Archive of Maryland Historical Photographs*, which is housed in the Maryland Hall of Records in Annapolis. Readers who desire to learn more about the state's heritage through early photographs are encouraged to investigate the collection.

Each section of this volume begins with a map that gives the position of each place illustrated in the photographs. To help our readers orient themselves, we have indicated some major highways even though these specific roads may not have existed before 1940. We also call attention to the map on page 168 which identifies many locations on the Chesapeake Bay and its tributaries.

MAME WARREN
MARION E. WARREN

Foreword

A Sense of Time and Place

BY EDWARD C. PAPENFUSE

Archivist and Commissioner of Land Patents for the State of Maryland

The importance of photographs as historical evidence was probably first recognized by lawyers who realized that a photograph could be an important component in stating a client's case simply and clearly. We have yet to identify the first Maryland court case in which photographs were used as evidence, but in inventorying the papers of the Baltimore City courts we found photographs of a Civil War soldier accused of bigamy; exterior and interior shots of a row house, circa 1910, documenting how well a son had cared for his mother before his sister had allegedly ''stolen'' her away; and many pictures of yellow taxi cabs, hand colored (in the days before color photography), perhaps meant to prove that one firm was copying another too closely.

Photographs have also been used as documentation in investigations of social conditions, the most famous being Jacob Riis's photo essays on tenements in New York. Photographs used for documentation of conditions in Baltimore appear in U.S. Document 599 (1909), Report of the President's Home Commission, and the Hall of Records has an exceptional early twentieth-century collection of photographs showing the deplorable state of county poor houses and state ''insane asylums.''

But if the courts and investigatory commissions recognized the evidentiary value of photographs from the earliest days of photography, systematic efforts at collecting and cataloging photographs as historical evidence for state, local, or family history (beyond rather cursory topic indexing or some indication of why a photograph was taken in the first place, for example, indexing by street name to document street repairs) have been neglected by most archives,

The second-earliest outdoor view taken in Maryland known to have survived is this daguerreotype of the Battle Monument in Baltimore made in 1846 by John Plumbe, Jr. The earliest photograph, taken in 1842 and owned by a private collector in New York, is of Baltimore's Washington Monument. Most of the early photographs were formal portraits. An outdoor view as clear as this one (and dated this early) is rare.

historical societies, and libraries. That is not to say that photographs are not important components of the collections of such institutions. Large collections of photographs are to be found in public libraries, but they are usually not very well described because detailed and consistent cataloging is simply too expensive and demands a professional level of expertise which most institutions cannot afford. Even where collections are to some degree indexed, however, cataloging has probably come too late to take advantage of the firsthand (or secondhand) knowledge of the donor. Often the specificity of the scene (who, where, why, and to a lesser extent, when) is either lost forever or its retrieval would be such a labor-intensive task as to put it beyond the pocketbooks of most institutions.

For images of the past before photographs we must rely upon words or drawings and paintings. The descriptive power of words is limited no matter how clever their author, and an artist's work, however faithfully rendered, invariably reflects the training and imagination of the artist as much as it does the reality of the people or the event depicted.

Photographs, like paintings, can be deliberately misleading and put a better face on the past than it ought to have. For example, a cursory review of the photographs submitted in divorce cases in the early decades of this century would leave the impression that all parties were well-dressed providers and happy homemakers. Nor are family photographs always accurate. Picnics, for example, were not always happy events. I remember being badly stung at one family reunion and suffering the humiliation of having two hundred relatives laugh at my plight as I ran for cover, a cloud of bees close behind—although even I tried to smile for the group photo, the only remaining evidence of the day's festivities.

Devoid of written explanation and even reflecting staged events, photographs do allow us to glimpse an exclusive past in a way no other images can. A volunteer guide at the

These fashionable ladies posed for a winter portrait for Boonsboro photographer C. D. Young c. 1905. How much more meaningful this image would be if the identity of the one and the story of the creation of the other were known. Relatives from an earlier generation often can help solve such mysteries if only we take the time to ask them.

Maryland Historical Society has been known to ask children what they *smell* in early photographs of Baltimore City docks. With photographs we can capture something of the "smell" of the past, a feel for "the way things really were," to borrow a phrase from the German historian Leopold Von Ranke. But when we have specific information about the photographs themselves, they become even more valuable as historical evidence. Take, for example, the exceptionally fine collections of photographs sampled in this book, which owe their preservation to the persistence and loving care of their owners. Because these photographs have been identified by those who preserved them, their importance as historical evidence is immeasurably augmented. A photograph of Coxey's army in 1894 is a case in point. Alone, it is a group shot of interesting faces with no connection to time, place, or event. Just the label "Coxey's Army, Cumberland, 1894," tells us something about the people we see. During the Depression of 1893, Jacob Sechler Coxey, of Massillon, Ohio, devised a plan to save the country from similar economic crises in the future. His scheme called for the government to print paper money to be spent on roads and other public improvements which would in turn create jobs for the unemployed. In 1894 he and a "human petition" of about one hundred men, known as "Coxey's Army," and a large number of reporters set out on a march to Washington which took them through Cumberland, Maryland, where this photograph was taken. With a label identifying who, what, why, and where, the photograph becomes useful historical evidence, not just a fascinating, detached, and unrelated image of the past.

The efforts of people like the Warrens to describe, catalog, and preserve have salvaged many photographs from relative obscurity. We all can learn a lesson from their work. Each of us needs to take time to identify the photographs we have and perhaps give some thought to writing brief descriptive labels for those photographs we will take in the future. Americans must spend almost as much time and money as the Japanese on photographic images of the world about them. Yet collections continue to arrive at the archives filled with photographs of nameless faces, places, and events. We are all familiar with the problem. Who doesn't have a bureau drawer full of photographs that he or she never quite got around to sorting out for that picture album there was never time to make?

When my great Aunt Sara died in 1971 at "an advanced age," she left me several albums and a trunk full of photographs. We had spent many winter nights in the early 1960s sorting out the pictures in the trunk, categorizing them as best we could by family subject then writing on the back the dates and the names of as many people as she could identify. Still, there were many people and scenes Aunt Sara could not recall or would "have to ask Pearl or Agnes" about that we never did identify because we never got around to taking the time, or by the time we asked, Pearl and Agnes had forgotten. For every photograph Aunt Sara and I talked about and cataloged, there were at least ten we could not, or did not get to, before she died—including one of Grandfather, perhaps taken when he was a law student, in costume holding a large teddy bear. The occasion has long since been forgotten (which, from the look on his face, would not have displeased Grandfather), and there is no one left to ask. But at least the photograph provides a human dimension to my image of someone I never knew.

To be useful as historical evidence photographs must be more than elusive images of forgotten relatives and scenes. Photographs, when clearly labeled and identified, can be evidence of what generations after about 1840 did, where they did it, and what it all looked like. Successive photographs taken from the dome of the Maryland State House document the construction of a frame house on North Street and reveal countless other details of change in the state capital. Successive family photographs tell us that Grandfather, too, was once young. A panoramic picture of the family farm taken in 1902 from the hill behind the barn is alive with outbuildings and implied prosperity. From the same vantage point today all one can see is the farmhouse and an overgrown berry patch where the shop used to be and the charred remains of the barn next to a crumbling silo, now unsafe to climb.

Food was abundant at the Swanger family picnic in Grantsville c. 1910, but the smiles were few.

Photographs provide a sense of time and place, frozen for posterity to imagine what things must have been like. For a photograph to be more, it must be related to other photographs or records in a way that either provides a historical context or tells a story, whether it be of a family, a place, or an event. This is what Mame and Marion Warren are doing so well in books like this and in their carefully cataloged photographic archives at the Maryland Hall of Records. There you will find what they could not use in this volume—an additional two thousand images—as closely identified as time and surviving memories would permit. It is hoped that this book and the archives from which it is derived will inspire others to do likewise, so that in the future, when we seek out the photographic evidence of our past, we will know what we see, who we see, and when it was seen, thus enabling us to have a much clearer perception of those who have preceded us and to whom we owe so much.

Introduction

Photographs Always Lie

BY WILLIAM STAPP

Curator of Photography, The National Portrait Gallery, Washington, D.C.

ew inventions in history have been adopted as quickly or as enthusiastically as was photography in 1839. In an age that measured civilization by technological progress, photography was seen as a culminating achievement of science, one that harnessed technology to make pictures whose detail and factuality surpassed that of those drawn or painted by the most talented artists. It is an indication of the force of this belief, first, that descriptions of the first photographic processes were disseminated world-wide in 1839 as quickly as the communications systems of the period allowed; second, that as soon as these descriptions became available anywhere, photographs were made; and third, that within less than a year of its introduction, photography was rapidly being transformed from an exciting scientific novelty into an industry and a profession. While this transformation occurred everywhere, it was particularly vigorous in the United States, so that by 1845 at the latest, there was a photographer (specifically, a daguerreotypist) in virtually every American town of any size and prosperity.

From the beginning, the documentary potential of photography was comprehended, even if it was expressed in exaggerated terms: *That light should be its own historian and draftsman, is, indeed, a sublime conception. . . . What would we now give to see before us the realities of past history—to see Jerusalem with its dazzling temple when it contained its nine millions of inhabitants—to see the encamped hosts of Israel, or to behold the city of the Caesars, or the armies of Alexander!* In fact, the earliest photographic processes, specifically the daguerreotype and the calotype, were inadequate, or at least unsuited, for this kind of documentation because they required extremely cumbersome equipment, were often inconsistent and un-

*"The Daguerreolite," Cincinnati *Daily Chronicle,* January 17, 1840.

Marketing techniques used by early photographers were often quite imaginative. This industrious camera artist set up shop on the Chesapeake & Ohio Canal in Cumberland c. 1890.

predictable in their results, and above all, required such long exposure times that a figure moving in the picture would be recorded as a blur or not at all. Indeed, with few exceptions, until the Civil War, photography in the United States was largely confined to the portrait studio, where the nonportability of the equipment was immaterial, where working conditions were reasonably controlled, and where the camera's subject could be immobilized with a neckbrace and backrest for the several seconds required to make the exposure.

Throughout most of the nineteenth century, American photography concentrated on portraiture, owing partly to the mechanical and chemical limitations of the photographic media then in use, which effectively restricted who could take photographs, but owing also to the social demand for portraits, which had a more profound emotional significance then than they do today.

As for the different media, it is essential to understand that until the late 1870s, when commercially manufactured sensitized glass plates (gelatine dry plates) became available, all photographs were entirely user made, usually on the spot. This was true for both the daguerreotype process, which dominated American photography from 1839 into the mid-to-late 1850s, and the so-called wet collodion process, which began to supersede the daguerreotype in the mid-1850s and in 1879 was rendered obsolete by the gelatine dry plate, the immediate ancestor of all modern photographic films. It is almost impossible to comprehend today, when photography has become miniaturized and almost completely automated, how physically difficult it was to make a photograph during, say, the Civil War, when the first extensive use was made of the camera in America to document comprehensively a major historical event as it occurred, in the field. During these years, the photographer carried all his equipment, including his darkroom, into the field in a wagon. To take a picture, he had to polish a sheet of glass until it was smooth, coat it evenly with collodion (a clear,

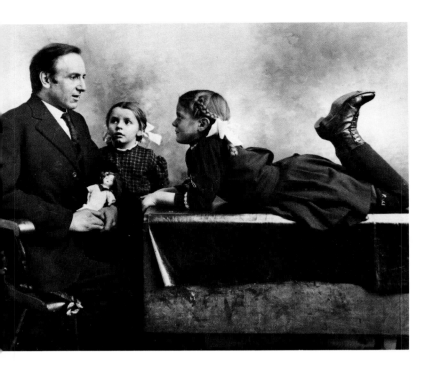

Photographer Leo J. Beachy posed for this charming self-portrait with his nieces "Sis" Beachy and Myra Custer c. 1915.

exposure times involved that nineteenth century likenesses are so sober and composed.

The revolution that occurred in photographic technology in the late 1870s and 1880s changed all this. Of major significance was the introduction of commercially manufactured photographic materials, which were consistent and reliable in their results and were more sensitive to light than anything previously available, and which freed the photographer from the absolute necessity of having a darkroom immediately at hand. Even more profound in its popular effect was the introduction, in 1888, of the Kodak camera, which completely eliminated the need for the photographer to have any technical expertise or ability. "You push the button, we do the rest," was Kodak's slogan, and this camera democratized photography, making picture-taking available to anyone who could afford it. It also introduced a spontaneity and immediacy to photography that has largely eroded, at least on the popular level, the sophisticated nineteenth-century understanding that photographs are historical documents, containing information as well as stimulating memories. The great proliferation of images this revolution in photographic technology has brought about has resulted in an enormous, ever-growing body of visual material, the historical value of which we are only beginning to appreciate and for which we are just beginning to develop the expertise and tools necessary for evaluation.

The photographs of Leo J. Beachy (1874–1927) exemplify both the intrinsic appeal of historical photographs and their inherent, but often decipherable, mystery. Taken during the first quarter of this century, they document the town, the people, and the surroundings of Grantsville, Maryland, the small hamlet where Beachy spent his entire life. They depict an idyllic, rural America, permeated with the sense of community and stability we idealize today. Beachy's photographs are entrancing pictures, composed with naive charm, reflecting the attitudes, expectations, and conventions of the photographer and his audience—his neighbors. Ironically, Beachy's photographs were taken under conditions of extreme hardship, for he suffered from a progressively degenerative muscular disease and could not walk or even stand without assistance.

It is important to remember, too, when looking at these photographs, that they are frequently topical—that is, they record some specific event—and that they were meant primarily for local consumption, so the significance of their subject matter was both obvious to and understood by their immediate audience. Because these meanings are largely hidden today (although they can, perhaps, be discovered), we tend to appreciate Beachy's photographs solely for their nostalgic content and esthetic quality. Even so, many of these pictures are compelling, summoning up visions of a style of life blessed by innocence, devoid of the anxieties of the modern urban world, unclouded by the omnipresent threat of global cataclysm. These photographs reflect a complete preoccupation with the local; in all of them, there is only one direct reference to external events: the sentimental piece, probably conceived as a post card, entitled "Love Waiteth for Your Return, My Soldier Boy."

tacky, viscous liquid made by dissolving guncotton in ether), sensitize it in a silver-nitrate bath, load it in the plate holder, insert it in the camera, make the exposure, and then return immediately to the darkroom to develop the plate *before it dried out*, otherwise the plate would be ruined. If the photographer was successful, he had a negative that could be used to make any number of prints; but he could not record action, nor could he photograph inconspicuously. It is understandable that during its first forty years, photography was restricted to professionals and to a few truly dedicated amateurs who had the leisure, the income, and the patience to devote themselves to their demanding hobby.

As for the importance of portraits, the nineteenth century was a period of extensive migration and high mortality rates. Separation, for whatever reason, was often permanent. In these circumstances, the photographic portrait—whether it were daguerreotype, tintype, ambrotype, or *carte de visite*—because it preserved the physical appearance of the person depicted, was invested with the almost mystical power of preserving their physical presence. Portraits of national figures, who were seen as the embodiments of the nation's spirit and character, were morally enlightening; portraits of family members and friends were *aides-mémoire* of incredible power. In both cases, the portraits were taken with a conscious awareness of posterity and were intended, first, to record the individual's features and appearance exactly; and, second, to suggest through pose and expression his or her character and proper moral fiber. *All our books, all our newspapers, all our private letters—though they are all to be weighed yearly by the ton rather than counted by the dozens—will not so betray us to our coming critics as the millions of photographs we shall leave behind us*—so wrote a critic for the *New York Times* in 1860. It is as much for this reason as it is for long

Like all photographs from the past, Leo J. Beachy's are historical documents. They faithfully record the appearance of Grantsville and its people and some of the events that occurred there over fifty years ago. They take us back through time and show us scenes from the past, as they actually were and—since we interpret them through our own sentiments and beliefs and memories—as they were not. In looking at these photographs, therefore, we must not take them at face value if we are truly to understand their historical meaning. They must be dissected, not as images, but as obscure texts that reflect fragmentary aspects of a specific society at a specific time. To understand them and to derive their meaning we must investigate their historical context in its entirety. That is a task beyond the scope of this introduction. But it should nonetheless be noted and understood that the fundamental nineteenth-century belief about photographs—a belief that Beachy himself inevitably shared—that it was, in effect, the unimpeachable witness, is inherently false. Photographs always lie: they record

Makeshift studio/darkrooms like this one in Cumberland were not at all unusual in the adventurous early days of photography. The man or woman with a camera had to have many talents and considerable physical strength to wield camera equipment, which was both heavy and bulky.

appearances only, and they are completely informed by all the conscious and unconscious attitudes and conceits of their makers. As documents, the closer they are to the event, the greater their informational impact. And as they age, they become pictures.

Beachy's photographs exemplify this process. We see them now largely as pictures that remind us of the past, if not as it actually was, then at least as we think it ought to have been. Even if we do not extract more profound or even ironic meaning from them, they reassure us about our past, and thus give us comfort for the present and for the future. That is no mean accomplishment for an unpretentious, small-town photographer.

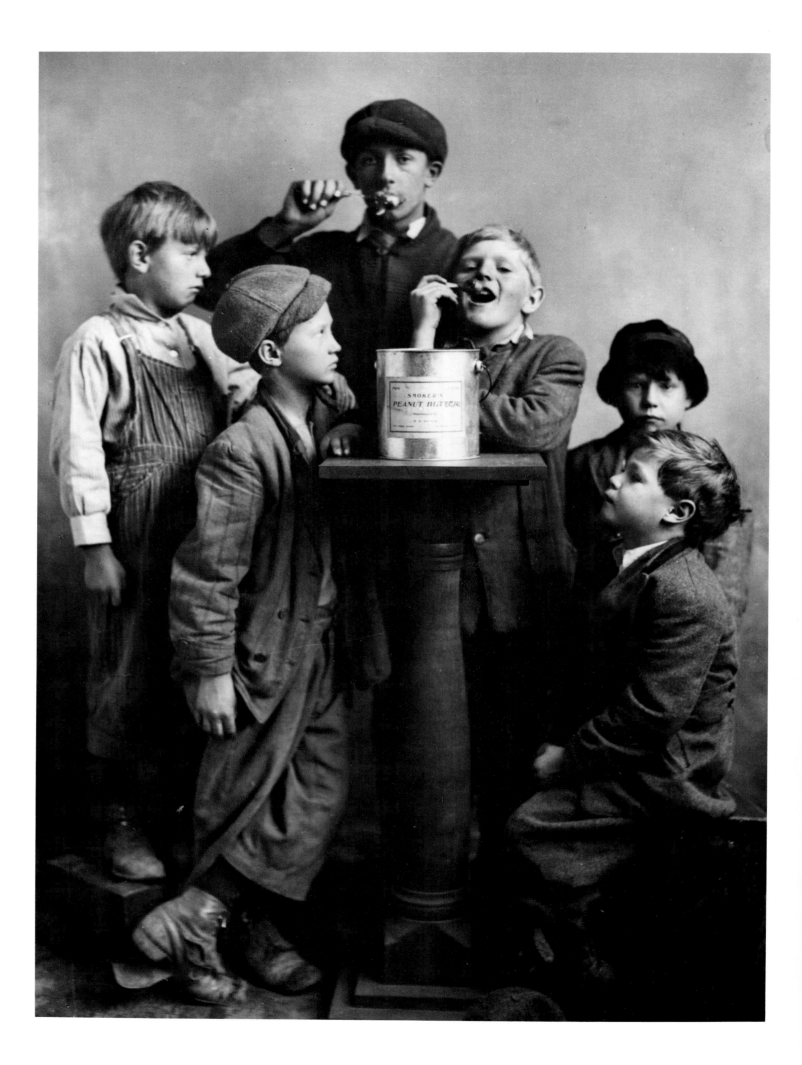

Acknowledgments

F ortune was with us time and again during the two years we researched and prepared *Maryland Time Exposures*. Generous friends—both new-found and well established—contributed grants, photographs, ideas, impressions, facts, and essays, all of which made this project possible and this book a reality. There are not enough synonyms to properly express our gratitude to those who participated in this project. If the following acknowledgments seem excessive, know that each person named gave uniquely and unselfishly and deserves mention.

Support for this project came from many quarters. We are grateful to Robert G. Merrick and the Jacob and Annita France Foundation and its staff; the Marion I. and Henry J. Knott Foundation; the Maryland Humanities Council; the Maryland Heritage Committee; the Chesapeake and Potomac Telephone Company of Maryland; Martin Marietta Corporation; Baltimore Gas and Electric Company; Mrs. Carlton Mitchell and Baltimore Federal Financial. We salute their willingness to invest in an idea and hope that they share our pride in its accomplishment.

As we traversed the state we were indeed lucky to locate a number of exceedingly rich caches of photographs in private collections. The individuals who carefully preserve these images are to be especially commended for their painstaking work. We are particularly grateful to the following friends for their trust and hospitality: in Easton, Michael Luby surprised us with an exceptional collection of post cards and stereographs, and Ebe Pope gave us access to the hundreds of post cards he has gathered since childhood; in Grantsville, Maxine Beachy Broadwater, custodian of the Leo J. Beachy negatives; in Cumberland, Mike Pearce, Gary Bartik, and Bill Demo introduced the Herman and Stacia Miller collection to us; in Baltimore, Elouise Harding, keeper of the Henry Rinn, Jr., collection, Jack and Beverly

Grantsville photographer Leo Beachy gathered his nephews for this deadpan publicity picture for Smoker's Peanut Butter c. 1920.

Wilgus—stereograph collectors extraordinaire, and Graham Wood, who has assembled thousands of items from the steamboat era; in Westminster, Raymond Hicks, who specialized in Western Maryland Railway memorabilia; in Cambridge, Hubert Wright IV shared the fruits of his own extensive research and Morley and Judy Jull loaned us precious glass-plate negatives; in New Market, Franklin Shaw delved into his storeroom to unearth his photographic treasures; in St. Mary's City, Burt Kummerow entrusted us with copy negatives from his files; in Hagerstown, John Frye welcomed us into the treasure-trove in the Western Maryland Room at the Washington County Free Library; in Boonsboro, Doug Bast made available the remarkable work of photographer C. D. Young; in Laurel, John Brennan offered the collection of photographer Robert Sadler; and in Talbot County, Dr. Laurence Claggett permitted us to copy from his impressive post-card collection.

Others who kindly provided photographs were Frederick Tilp, Dan Toomey, William Hollifield, A. N. Miller, Ross Kelbaugh, Leroy Merrikew, Kenneth Kaumeyer, Josie Lines, Virginia Turner Somerville, William Wimbrow, Harry Jones, Frances Potter, Margaret Estlow, Nita Burdette, Enalee Bounds, Harriet Welch, Polly Barber, Mildred Kemp, Paul Randall, Mrs. William Rowe, Hilda Cushwa, Marguerite Doleman, Mary Middleton White, Robert and Rob Withey, Lois Harrison, Katherine Etchison, Jack Mellin, Tish Dryden, and Peter Tasi.

Volunteers and the staffs of county and local historical societies were more than gracious in receiving us and our camera. Particular thanks are due to Rita Knox in Allegany County; Ora and John Smith in Anne Arundel County; Alain Dessaint and Tom Wisner of the Southern Maryland Today project in Calvert County; JoAnn Manwaring and Helen Riley in Carroll County; Phyllis Hurd and Mary Semey Schmidt in Cecil County; Irene Harper in Dorchester County; Judith Proffitt in Frederick County; Mary Love in Garrett County; Mary Wright and Clark Jones in Harford County; Marie Zimmer, Mari Lewin Handwerk, and Anita

Cushing in Howard County; Beppie and Bob Bryan in Kent County; Jane Sween in Montgomery County; Alan Virta, Fred DeMarr, John Walton, Jr., and Cathy Wallace in Prince George's County; Elizabeth Flower and Mary Elizabeth Abel in Queen Anne's County; Norman Harrington and Georgia Adler in Talbot County; Charles Lyon, Ralph Donnelly, Marge Peters, Nellie Reed, and Rhoda Bowers in Washington County; Art Goetz in Wicomico County; Ed Hammond and Kathy Fisher in Worcester County; and Bettsie Miller of the Columbia Historical Society in Washington, D. C.

Other organizations played a major role in supplying images for this volume. We wish to acknowledge the professional and personal attention we were given by Alyce Libby, Phebe Jacobsen, and Jane McWilliams of the Maryland Hall of Records; Oliver Jensen, Leroy Bellamy, and Mary Ison of the Prints and Photographs Division of the Library of Congress; Edward Earle of the California Museum of Photography at Riverside; Ross Kimmel of the Department of Natural Resources; Tom Beck of the Edward L. Bafford Photography Collection at the University of Maryland, Baltimore County; Geoffrey W. Fielding, Carol Pollack, Alice Martin, and Lisa Vickari of the Baltimore County Public Library; Morgan Pritchett of the Maryland Department of the Enoch Pratt Free Library; Laurie Baty of the Department of Prints and Photographs of the Maryland Historical Society; Peter Liebhold of the Baltimore Museum of Industry; Richard Bonney and Barnard Tarleton of the Printing and Photographic Services of Baltimore Gas and Electric Company; John Schisler of the Chesapeake and Potomac Telephone Company; Martin R. Jones of the Charles County Extension Office; Nancy Brennan and Richard W. Flint of the Peale Museum; Wayne Asplen of the Dorchester County Health Department; Mrs. David Witt of the Susquehanna Museum of Havre de Grace; Jessie Hinkle and Donald Farren of Special Collections, University of Maryland, College Park Libraries; Ivy Carter of the Thurgood Marshall Library at Bowie State College; Richard L. Stanton and Lee Struble of the Chesapeake & Ohio Canal National Historic Park; Suzanne B. Hurley of the Ocean City Life-Saving Station Museum; Bernard Loveless of the Chesapeake Beach Railway Museum; and Mike W. Delano and Thel Hauck of the Worcester County Extension Office.

Good ideas and suggestions for potential picture sources were plentiful and many led to particularly rich collections. For their recommendations and input we thank Mary Blair and Elinor Sklar of the Maryland Humanities Council; Jack Carr of the Department of Economic and Community Development; Frank Hopkins of Maryland My Maryland; Keith Richwine of Western Maryland College; Kristi Eisen-

berg and William Short of Cecil County Community College; Constance Stapleton; Marianne Alexander of Goucher College; George Calcott of the University of Maryland; Douglass and Paula Reed; and Dave Cottingham.

We are grateful to Will Stapp, Curator of Photography at the National Portrait Gallery, for lending his expertise and greatly enhancing the thoroughness of this volume with his introduction.

Several persons have played major roles by championing this project and helping to bring it to fruition.

Nancy Essig, regional book editor of the Johns Hopkins University Press, conceived the idea of producing a comprehensive photographic history of the state as a contribution to the celebration of the 350th anniversary of the founding of Maryland. Her constant encouragement and enthusiasm have inspired us from the beginning. Among the extremely helpful staff members at the Johns Hopkins University Press, several people deserve special thanks: Jack Goellner and Arlene Sullivan continually came to our aid in times of frustration, Hazel Sarigianis never lost a message, and Mary Lou Kenney polished the manuscript and proposed many helpful and insightful alterations.

Gerard A. Valerio is responsible for much of the pleasure our readers will experience as they turn these pages. In our opinion, Gerry Valerio is a designer of consummate sensitivity and skill. His thoughtful review of the many hundreds of photographs accumulated helped us to make intelligent and often difficult choices. Then, like a wizard, he gently molded and crafted our selections into an agreeable whole.

Flora P. Chambers had the thankless job of cataloging the thousands of negatives that were produced in this project. More times than we like to admit she kept the chaos from overwhelming us, and her good humor sustained our spirits.

Edward C. Papenfuse contributed much more to this effort than his excellent foreword. From the outset he has been an untiring advocate of our work. His recognition of the importance of preserving the images we acquired under archival conditions gave us added incentive to be as thorough as possible in our research. Time and again he gave us the moral support we needed to continue what seemed a never-ending task. Special mention should also be made of Susan Cummings's careful management of *The Robert G. Merrick Archive of Maryland Historical Photographs* at the Hall of Records. Her diligence in sorting through hundreds of prints and negatives is remarkable and most appreciated.

Finally, for their unfaltering patience and understanding, we thank our dear families. Mary G. Warren, Henry Harris, and Rodney Harris have been the best of friends.

M.W. AND M.E.W.

Maryland

TIME EXPOSURES

1840-1940

EASTERN Maryland

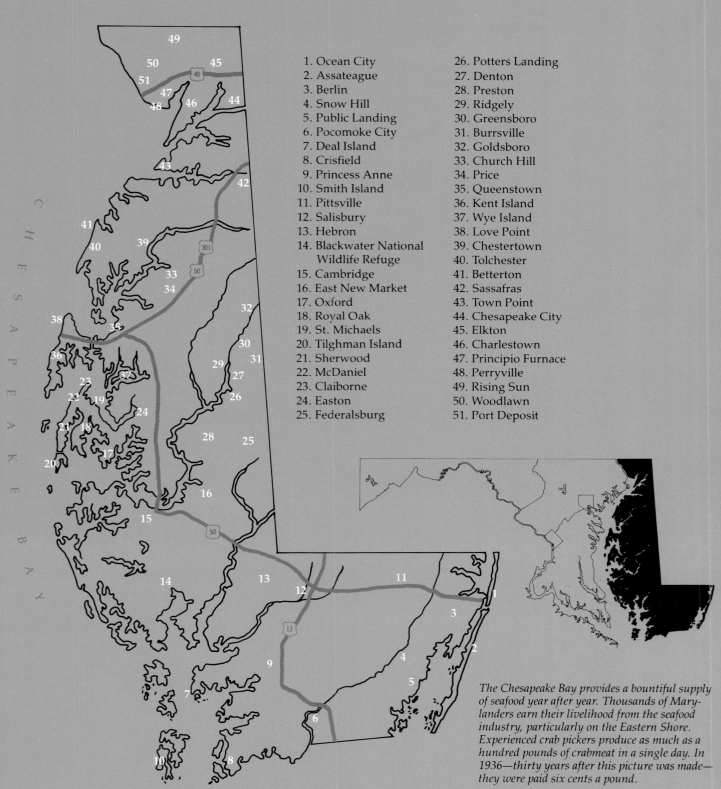

1. Ocean City
2. Assateague
3. Berlin
4. Snow Hill
5. Public Landing
6. Pocomoke City
7. Deal Island
8. Crisfield
9. Princess Anne
10. Smith Island
11. Pittsville
12. Salisbury
13. Hebron
14. Blackwater National Wildlife Refuge
15. Cambridge
16. East New Market
17. Oxford
18. Royal Oak
19. St. Michaels
20. Tilghman Island
21. Sherwood
22. McDaniel
23. Claiborne
24. Easton
25. Federalsburg
26. Potters Landing
27. Denton
28. Preston
29. Ridgely
30. Greensboro
31. Burrsville
32. Goldsboro
33. Church Hill
34. Price
35. Queenstown
36. Kent Island
37. Wye Island
38. Love Point
39. Chestertown
40. Tolchester
41. Betterton
42. Sassafras
43. Town Point
44. Chesapeake City
45. Elkton
46. Charlestown
47. Principio Furnace
48. Perryville
49. Rising Sun
50. Woodlawn
51. Port Deposit

The Chesapeake Bay provides a bountiful supply of seafood year after year. Thousands of Marylanders earn their livelihood from the seafood industry, particularly on the Eastern Shore. Experienced crab pickers produce as much as a hundred pounds of crabmeat in a single day. In 1936—thirty years after this picture was made— they were paid six cents a pound.

Ocean City, the state's only port directly on the Atlantic Ocean, has long been a favorite vacation spot for Marylanders. The first hotel, the Atlantic, opened in 1875. Fishing is a popular sport there (note the pound fishing boats pulled up on the sand in the view at right taken c. 1900). Marlin fishing became fashionable after a hurricane in 1933 reopened an inlet south of town giving access to a safe harbor on Sinepuxent Bay.

When photographer H. Robins Hollyday took this aerial view in the 1930s, Ocean City was less than three miles long. The quarter-mile-wide sandy barrier reef on which the city stands is separated from the rest of Worcester County by a narrow arm of Sinepuxent Bay.

Weather has not always been kind to Ocean City. The railroad that once brought throngs from inland cities was destroyed by the 1933 hurricane. By that time, however, automobiles had replaced trains as the preferred mode of transportation for most. This photograph records the damage suffered by the boardwalk during a 1936 storm.

By 1940 the boardwalk was two miles long and huge crowds were making regular weekend jaunts from Baltimore and Washington, D.C. Frank Socca's band entertained the modestly dressed multitude.

FOLLOWING PAGES:
The popularity of this physical fitness class on the beach suggests that the current health fad may not be so newfangled after all.

5

In 1936, when this uncooperative pony was being loaded onto a ferry, the "wild" ponies of Assateague were carefully monitored and new blood was introduced into the herd every other year. At that time, the island was owned by a woman who lived in Baltimore.

There are four Trappes in Maryland, and three are on the Eastern Shore. The one below, a hamlet near Berlin in Worcester County, is located at the head of Trappe Creek. There was once a gristmill here, but trade declined as the town of Berlin grew prosperous in the nineteenth century.

Worcester County boasts some of Maryland's richest farmland. These local youngsters were well on their way as the next generation of farmers in Berlin when they climbed aboard their Field Day float in 1920.

Harrison's was for many years the largest employer in Berlin. Founded in 1884, the fruit tree nursery was once the largest in the world, with more than five thousand acres under cultivation in Maryland. In 1928 Mr. Harrison and some of his workers paused from their picking in the Elberta peach orchard to pose for a picture, below.

There was a big turnout on April 4, 1908, when the citizens of Berlin officially voted to ban the sale of alcoholic beverages. In a resolution passed the previous month, the citizenry had declared that ''our best interests are affected by the continued sale of intoxicants to our people, that continued indulgence in it tends to poverty, degradation and crime, that it entails on our descendants ignorance, dwarfed intellect and moral degeneracy, that it dissipates success, fortune and virtue, that it lowers the standard of civilization and corrupts the ballot, that it strangles justice and menaces liberty, that our reason, observation and experience all teach us that it is the greatest evil of our age and that majority rule is both reasonable and just.''

9

The Worcester County seat, Snow Hill, is located on the Pocomoke River, which is navigable up to this point. Although much of the business district was destroyed by a fire in 1893, most of the town, settled in 1642, retains its historic charm.

Harness racing has long been a popular sport in Maryland. It was neck and neck at this event at the Snow Hill Fairgrounds, c. 1915.

Public Landing was once a favorite summer resort on Chincoteague Bay with a hotel, private cottages, and amusements. Until the railroads came, Public Landing was a busy shipping point for freight being transported overland to Snow Hill.

The lower Eastern Shore is chiefly occupied with truck farming. Crops include tomatoes, melons, kale, broccoli, spinach, soybeans, and potatoes. These strawberries—grown, sorted, and packed in Worcester County—were shipped to markets all over Maryland and the Northeast.

Worcester and Somerset counties yield most of Maryland's annual potato crop. An exceptionally mild climate permits 210 growing days each year, enough to allow two separate plantings. At left, Charles Chesser and his workers demonstrate an up-to-date sweet potato transplanter in 1925.

Pocomoke City, located twelve miles southwest of Snow Hill on the Pocomoke River, is the commercial center of Worcester County. Although the town—first called Meeting House Landing—was established about 1700, there are virtually no structures left from those early days. Three disastrous fires, in 1888, 1892, and 1922, caused property damages valued in millions of dollars. This view of Front and Market streets was published as a picture post card c. 1909.

Pocomoke City was on the Pennsylvania Railroad line. The sign on the train station behind the band members pictured here proclaims the name by which the town is usually known—Pocomoke. "City" is rarely uttered by locals.

May Day 1912 inspired this frolicking celebration of spring by the students of Pocomoke High School.

The date of this photograph, March 21, 1908—just two weeks before Berlin voted to go dry—suggests that the occasion for this gathering of women and children in Pocomoke might have been related to prohibition.

Deal Island is located on Tangier Sound. Its inhabitants have long made their living almost exclusively from the seafood industry. Work boats line the harbor; millions of oysters are shucked and crabs picked in local packing houses. In 1938, two million soft-shell crabs were packed alive in wet grass and shipped to Northern cities from the island.

13

Crisfield has dubbed itself the Seafood Capital of the Nation, and with good reason. These crab pickers worked at Milbourne Oyster Company c. 1940. In Crisfield, oyster boats known elsewhere in Maryland as skipjacks are called bateaux.

In 1868 John W. Crisfield brought the railroad to town, and the resulting prosperity inspired the citizens to rename Somers Cove in his honor. Train tracks run down the middle of South Main Street, right out to the water's edge, enabling refrigerated cars to be loaded directly from the work vessels that deliver crabs, oysters, and fish. This aerial, taken c. 1935, views the harbor and town.

Part of Business Section

Princess Anne Md.

Smith Island's reputation for remoteness and a unique character is well deserved. Named for Captain John Smith who explored the Chesapeake in 1608, the island has been settled since the mid-seventeenth century. By 1850 every Smith Islander had converted to Methodism, and religion became the focal point of life. The populace believed that God had given oysters, crabs, fish, and waterfowl as a gift to them and did not take kindly to government restrictions on duck hunting and oyster dredging. Similarly, they chose to build and maintain their own roads, so no vehicles on the island bear license plates. The view of Tylerton, above, one of three communities on the island, was taken in 1939.

Princess Anne, the seat of Somerset County, was named in honor of the daughter of King George II. The Washington Hotel on U.S. Route 13 has been in business since the colonial period. As recently as 1900 schooners sailed up the Manokin River to deliver and receive goods. Since then the river bed has gradually filled with silt from shoreline farm erosion and the Manokin is now unnavigable by large craft.

15

PRECEDING PAGES:

For many years Pittsville boasted the largest auction block for strawberries in Wicomico County. This photograph was taken at the height of the strawberry season in 1910. The town was originally known as Derrickson's Cross Roads, but when the Wicomico and Pocomoke Railroad came in 1868, the town was renamed for Dr. Hilary R. Pitts of Berlin, president of the railroad.

Salisbury suffered several disastrous fires in the nineteenth century. The tintype at right, taken c. 1856, may be the only remaining photograph of the city before the fire of 1860. The view was made at the corner of Main and Division streets. Originally, the city was partly in Somerset and partly in Worcester County—hence the name Division Street. Salisbury is the largest city on the Eastern Shore.

When Wicomico County was established in 1867, Salisbury was named the county seat. The great fire of 1886 burned the heart of the commercial district: the town hall, opera house, churches, post office, fifty-five stores, fifty-eight homes, four stables, two hotels, a bank, and the newspaper office were all destroyed. The view above was taken from Camden Bridge.

The Wicomico County courthouse was the one public building that survived the fire. The bell from St. Peter's Episcopal Church, which sounded the first alarm, was installed in the courthouse tower to announce the hours.

Santa Claus arrived early for Christmas in Salisbury in 1911. Since the advent of the automobile, Salisbury has been the commercial center for the lower Eastern Shore.

F. A. Grier & Son was a machine works located on the Wicomico River, which provided easy access for the many boats serviced. Mr. Grier first came to Salisbury as a firefighter from Wilmington during the 1886 conflagration. His son was Wicomico County's first fire marshal.

The citizens of Salisbury turned out in style to celebrate the election of Woodrow Wilson.

A beauty pageant held in Salisbury in July 1940 attracted a large crowd of spectators.

When the Baltimore, Chesapeake and Atlantic Railway built its station in Hebron in 1890, there was just one house and a store there. By 1914, when the photograph at left was taken, a considerable town had evolved, thanks to the presence of the rail line.

Eventually, Hebron became Wicomico County's fourth largest community.

A wide creek divides the Dorchester County seat into East and West Cambridge. When a long freeze settled in on Cambridge Creek c. 1910, skaters came out in droves to enjoy the situation. Each evening the Rescue Fire Company hosed down the creek to make the surface smooth.

Cambridge is the Eastern Shore's second largest city in both size and commercial activity. After the Civil War numerous businesses—including saw, flour, and textile mills, shipyards, canneries, and a fertilizer plant—were established to serve the surrounding community. With the increasing population, Charles Dill undoubtedly shoed many a horse at his blacksmith shop.

Migratory waterfowl find Maryland a favorite winter resort. In Dorchester County, where the cabin far left was located, an eight-thousand-acre marsh was established as the Blackwater Migratory Bird Refuge in 1931 by the federal government.

23

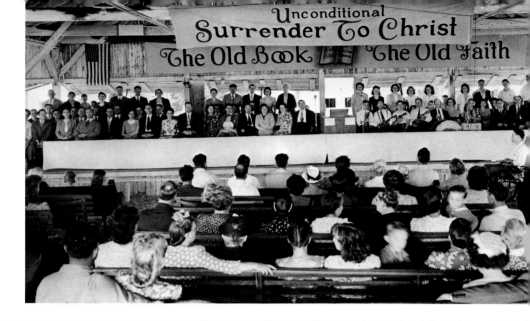

Participants in a revival camp meeting held in Cambridge c. 1940 were continuing a long tradition of religious involvement among Marylanders.

Cambridge is situated on the southern shore of the two-mile-wide Choptank River. This aerial view was made c. 1940.

By 1911 new modes of transportation were coming into style. This scene in front of the Phillips Hardware Company at the corner of Muir and Race streets illustrates the changing times.

24

The Brown Building in Cambridge was an outstanding example of Victorian architecture. Businesses located there provided for almost every worldly need: clothing, furniture, carpets, fabrics—and funerals.

Cambridge has been the seat of Dorchester County since 1686. Business at the courthouse, as well as Cambridge's strategic location, made the city a logical stopping point for travelers. Hotel Dorchester, Hotel Cambridge, and the Oakley Beach Hotel, pictured at left, provided accommodations for visitors.

25

The Dorchester County Fair was held each August at the fairgrounds on Race Street Extended in Cambridge. Originally organized as social events, county fairs quickly developed into showplaces for the latest in agricultural technology and advances in growing and breeding techniques. The midway at the county fair c. 1911 afforded suppliers an opportunity to demonstrate their goods and services.

The photograph at left of the hotel that once stood on Sharps Island was a rare find: as a result of erosion, the island itself, once located at the mouth of the Choptank River, no longer exists.

Once a thriving fishing village, East New Market became the center of a productive farming community with easy access to both water and rail transportation.

The Maryland Oyster

from *The Book of the Royal Blue,* November 1898

W here the St. Michael and Choptank Rivers placidly flow into the Chesapeake Bay, and in the deep recesses of Tangier and Pocomoke Sounds, along the eastern shore of Maryland, hundreds of canoes and bateaus now ply the waters, manned by sturdy fishermen; for the oyster season, one of Maryland's greatest industries, has begun.

When September, the first month of the ''r'' is ushered in, the innumerable pleasure crafts which have plied these same waters from May until August, seek their winter moorings and give way entirely to the less ostentatious but more business-like fishing boats.

The method of taking the oyster from its home in the depths is interesting. Although the Tangier and Pocomoke Sounds and Choptank and St. Michael Rivers are favorite grounds for oystering in Maryland, the industry is extensively carried on throughout the lower Chesapeake Bay and rivers tributary thereto. Hundreds of sloops and small boats ply the waters, some anchored and some under slow motion, and these comprise the famous Maryland Oyster Navy.

The small craft, such as canoes and bateaus, are manned by two or more fishermen, who make a business of oystering eight months of the year. These men are known as ''tongers.'' Their implements

Oyster boats were locked into a frozen Cambridge Creek when the photograph at left was made. The Phillips Packing Company, in East Cambridge, was founded in 1902 to shuck oysters for northern markets. In later years the company added vegetables, meat, and fish to its product line. By 1940 the firm employed more than four thousand persons during peak seasons, and seven hundred the year round.

The oyster has been a Maryland delicacy from the beginning. Family oyster roasts, like this one in Talbot County c. 1895, are a time-honored tradition.

consists of a pair of ''tongs,'' similar in appearance to two hay rakes, with the prongs facing, fastened to poles ranging from 15 to 24 feet in length. Each pair of tongs requires two persons to manipulate it. The size of the catch depends upon the strength of the tongers. When the oysterman locates his fishing ground, he anchors his canoe and the great tongs are immersed to the bed of the river. The handles are forced apart and the two men manipulating them push forward toward each other, closing the prongs of the tongs together, scraping up the oysters on the bed. Then the tongs are lifted and contents dumped into what is called a ''culling board.'' The culling board is very similar to a sieve, the apertures of

which being about two and a half inches in diameter, the regulation requirement by law. All of the oysters which do not fall through the apertures are placed in the boat, while those which pass through the meshes are thrown back into the water.

When the canoes and bateaus are filled to their capacity, the fishermen take their cargo and dispose of it to the nearest ''pungy.'' A pungy is a large sloop, which anchors in the midst of an oyster fleet and receives the cargo of the smaller craft. While there are many firms which regularly hire a number of the fishermen in small craft to work for them alone, yet there are numbers of ''free-booters,'' who gather their wares and sell for the best price. When a pungy has its full load, it proceeds at once to Baltimore, from which point the oysters are shipped throughout the United States.

While tonging is the initiative method of oystering, it does not continue extensively when the extreme cold weather sets in, and it is then that dredging is the process most generally pursued. An oyster dredger commonly consists of a sloop, which is provided with two dredging machines in the center of the boat, one on each side. Each machine requires four to five men to operate it, and consists of a pair of heavy steel tongs three feet in width, supplemented at the back with a large wire basket, so that the oysters which are grappled rapidly by the tongs are forced back into the wire basket by the motion of the boat, which is under sail. When the basket is filled it is brought to the surface by means of a windlass and the contents disposed of on the culling board. The culling process is then gone through with the same as in the small boats.

By 1940 oysters made up 75 percent of the 40 million pounds of shellfish taken from the Chesapeake Bay annually. There are several methods for harvesting oysters. Tonging, shown here c. 1938, is the process used in water up to ten- or twelve-feet deep.

The laws governing tonging and dredging are very strict, and as the fishing grounds for each method are separated, a heavy fine is imposed for the trespassing of one upon the other.

The life of the oysterman is anything but an easy one. Many of the men who ply their business at oystering in winter, work at truck gardening in the summer time. If the man is going into the business as a tonger he is required to pay a license of $3.75 for the season. This license he is required to have with him and show to any Government official who demands it before he can enter the oyster fields, as the territory for oystering in Maryland is confined to certain limits. The man who hires himself out as a dredger receives anywhere from $20.00 to $30.00 per month for his services. He is generally hired by the captain of a sloop, who pays a dredger's license of $2.85 gross per ton. As the law governing the size of oysters which are marketable is a very strict one, a state inspector examines every load, and fishermen are allowed 5% of their cargo for such small oysters as they have on board which have not slipped through the culling board. Should the oysterman's cargo consist of more than 5% of small oysters, he is fined accordingly and possibly subjected to imprisonment as the case merits.

The oyster was known to the Indians as a sea food long before Columbus discovered the new world, and they were adepts in catching them. The oysters were a commodity of trade between the coast Indians and those living farther back in the interior.

It is not to be supposed, however, that oyster beds naturally grow from year to year supplying the endless demands. Their sources of supply are natural beds,

By law, oysters may be dredged from the deeper waters of the Chesapeake Bay and its tributaries only from vessels powered by sail. Specially designed scoops are lowered from skipjacks like these to dredge up the oysters from their beds on the Bay floor.

planting and farming. Oyster planting consists of placing the young seed oysters upon bottoms favorable for their growth. Oyster farming is the rearing of oysters from the egg. The natural bed is an oyster rock. In such a bed it will be found that most of the rock is made up of empty shells. The oysters grow vertically side by side, and the closeness is often so great that the growth of one oyster prevents adjacent ones from opening their shells and thus crowding each other out, they die. The most prolific beds for young oysters are the spaces intervening between the oyster rocks. For miles and miles along the edge of the shore can be found these oyster rocks, but between these beds there are areas where not a single oyster is to be found, and it is this barren area which is best adapted for oyster farming. After a few bushels of shells are scattered upon these areas they are soon covered with young, and in several years a new oyster rock is found.

The waters for miles around the natural bed are alive with young oysters, which are small animals, so small, indeed, that they can not be seen without the aid of a microscope. So it is when the shells are placed in the barren areas, the spat young ones cling to them.

In oyster planting clean oyster shells are placed upon bottoms just before the spawning season for attachment of the young, and among the shells are a few natural oysters to furnish the eggs. When the young ones are large enough they are distributed over the bottom. Of the millions of seed oysters which are planted annually at Wellfleet, Mass.; Portsmouth, N. H.; Portland, Me.; Buzzard Bay and Vineyard Sound, Narragansett Bay, in eastern Connecticut and in New York and Delaware Bays, fully one-half are taken from Maryland waters in Chesapeake Bay, and cost the planter less than twenty-five cents per bushel put down upon his beds. These oysters can be taken up within three or four months, at which time they are sold for more than eighty cents per bushel.

Baltimore is the home of the oyster trade, inasmuch as all the oysters taken from the Chesapeake Bay and the rivers tributary thereto are shipped to that port. The Maryland output alone is equivalent to any five of the other states. The oyster industry is the means of giving employment to thousands of men and thousands of dollars yearly to transportation lines, as the states throughout the Union are supplied principally with Maryland oysters.

Each succeeding year finds the industry branching out extensively, and it is needless to say that the Maryland oyster will require no emblazoned shaft to mark its memory.

It is unusual for work boats to dock with their sails hoisted. The captains of these skipjacks were probably trying to dry the canvas.

Oysters are in season from September to April—all the months that contain the letter r. During the cruel months of December, January, and February waters are often frozen over. These watermen braved the weather and cut through the ice to obtain their prey.

PRECEDING PAGES:
Boatbuilding is carried on in many locations on the Eastern Shore. The Oxford Boatyard Co., pictured in an aerial taken c. 1940, constructed many pleasure craft for sailors.

The Oxford-Bellevue Ferry is reputed to be the oldest free-running ferry in the United States. It crosses the Tred Avon River, which empties into the Choptank.

Oxford rivaled Annapolis as Maryland's busiest port in the eighteenth century. Called the Riverview when the photograph above was made in 1911, this handsome structure was allowed to fall into disrepair for some years. It has been restored as the Robert Morris Inn, named in honor of the one-time resident who served as agent of finance during the American Revolution.

Oxford is located on the southern tip of a peninsula; from the end of the village the Chesapeake Bay can be seen. Fishing, oyster, and pleasure boats are protected in a land-locked harbor.

The caption for the photograph at left of a ferry crossing the Miles River in 1913 is "a cause for profanity." The Miles River was originally called the St. Michaels, but the local Quaker settlers caused the Saint to be dropped and the name evolved into Miles.

The Pasadena in Royal Oak attracted a good clientele in the summer of 1910, below. The name of the village was derived from an incident during the War of 1812. When the British attacked the town of St. Michaels, a cannonball missed its mark and was lodged in a giant oak tree.

St. Michaels was once a great shipbuilding center; many clipper ships were launched from here, though Baltimore received the credit for them. Normally a quiet village, St. Michaels becomes a bustling port when the Miles River Regatta, in which many native Bay vessels compete, takes place. Perhaps it was just such an occasion that drew this crowd to the local train station.

St. Michaels is almost surrounded by water. The footbridge below led to an area called the peninsula where a crab house was located.

Crab picking, oyster shucking, fishing, truck farming, and working in canneries were the occupations most often available to blacks on the Eastern Shore prior to 1940—and for years thereafter, as well. This scene, described as "the hut of an oyster fisherman—Chesapeake Bay near Sherwood" was published as a stereograph by the Keystone View Company in 1905.

Tilghman Island is at the tip of Talbot County, reaching out into the Chesapeake Bay. Three-and-a-half miles long, the island contains three villages—Tilghman, Avalon, and Fairbank. Most inhabitants make their living from fishing, crabbing, and oystering. The long wharf seen at left was for steamboat landings.

At one time the Maryland shoreline was dotted with hundreds of guest houses where city dwellers escaped for a few days, weeks, or even an entire summer by the Bay. Wade's Point, near McDaniel, far left, enjoyed a loyal clientele for many years.

Although McDaniel was a tiny community, the Baltimore, Chesapeake and Atlantic Railway station there was obviously a busy place in 1910.

Claiborne was established by the Baltimore & Eastern Shore Railroad in 1886 as a ferry point on its line. It is well remembered as the terminus for the last ferry across the Bay, which traveled from Annapolis to Claiborne by way of Matapeake. These happy swimmers were guests at Maple Hall Farm, located at Claiborne.

Easton is described in the Tourists' Guide for Pleasure Trips to the Summer Resorts, Sea Bathing and Watering Places Convenient to Baltimore and Its Vicinity *(published in 1878) as "one of the most fashionable places on the Eastern Shore, a centre of wealth, gaiety and culture." No doubt some of those tourists, guidebooks in hand, stayed at the Brick Hotel, pictured at right in 1880.*

Easton is one of the few major towns on the Shore not located directly on the water. The headwaters of both the Tred Avon and Miles rivers are very near, however, and so the community, including Mr. Carpenter's Fish Market, is easily supplied with an abundance of fresh seafood.

The first car over the Baltimore, Chesapeake and Atlantic Railway arrived at Easton in 1886. The remainder of the line was not yet completed.

Hughes Drugstore seems to have had a remedy for every ailment when this portrait of the proprietors was made in 1896.

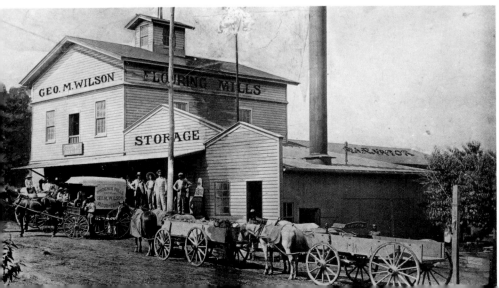

The Phoenix Flour Mill, operated by George Wilson, was a prosperous establishment in Easton in 1902.

41

The newspaper reported on September 27, 1919, that "last Saturday night the crowds in Easton were so large that comment was general. There were 314 cars actually counted, and if each of them brought five persons—and some brought more—there were 1,570 persons in town from the outlying districts. Money was freely spent, giving lie to the tales of hard times caused by poor crops. An effort was made to get the number of ice cream cones sold and the number of bottles of soft drinks. The former was impossible, as there was no way to check up other than the number of gallons of cream disposed of, and from this source it might be estimated that a thousand cones disappeared. As to the soft drinks, the truck loads of empty bottles being hauled away Monday morning is the best index."

A newspaper clipping c. 1915 boasted that Easton supported three banks, two building and loan associations, two good hotels, a fine high school, thirteen churches, three big canneries, the largest furniture store on the peninsula, a wholesale grocery house, and three moving picture theaters.

On market days the square in front of the court house would fill up with vendors selling vegetables and baked goods. The newspaper reported c. 1915 that "the police had to take control and indicate parking spaces. All four sides of the courthouse square were lined and the east side of Washington Street for three squares." The narrow shed pictured at right was the city's first public telephone booth.

42

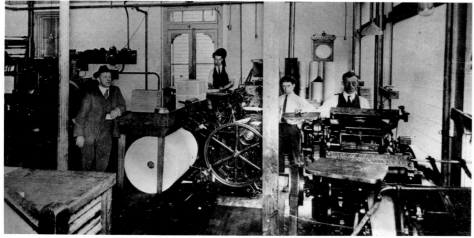

Easton supported three weekly newspapers early in this century. Workers on the presses at the Star Democrat *are pictured at left.*

A modest crowd turned out for the parade held on Washington Street on July 5, 1920. Much of Easton's social life was centered on the Chesapeake Bay Yacht Club.

Federalsburg assumed its name in 1812 when a mass meeting of the Federalist party was held there. Prior to that it was known as Northwest Fork Bridge. Although the lack of automobiles suggests that the photograph of Main Street, right, was taken earlier, the date on the original post card is 1915.

Although it becomes quite narrow, the Choptank river is navigable for many miles. The only inland county on the Eastern Shore—Caroline County—depends on the river for access to the Chesapeake Bay. This wharf, located five miles below Denton, was originally known as Potter's Landing. In 1847 the estate was purchased by a Mr. Willis who attempted to change the name to Williston, which is what it was called on a 1906 map of steamboat landings published by the B C & A Railway Company.

Apparently the convertible was the prevalent style for early automobiles in Denton.

The message on this post card of the Baltimore & Eastern Shore Railroad station at Preston, below, reads: ''This is the excursion crowd May 12, 1909.''

Denton was initially called Eden Town to honor Sir Robert Eden, the last colonial governor of Maryland and husband of Lady Caroline Calvert for whom the county was named. Lady Caroline was the sister of the last Lord Baltimore. The town's name was contracted to Edenton, then in 1791, when it was designated the county seat, the E was dropped and it became Denton. Denton was devastated by a fire that resulted from a tragic Fourth of July celebration in 1865. When the fireworks supply gave out, local boys began batting about lighted balls of candle wicks; one lodged on a roof and before long the entire business district was gone. The view of Main Street at left was made c. 1908.

Located on the Delaware and Chesapeake Railroad, Ridgely developed into an important forwarding point for farm products, particularly strawberries. The Armour Company opened a plant for making strawberry preserves. Several vegetable canneries operated here, as well as a factory for manufacturing crates, baskets, and strawberry boxes.

The local ratcatcher had a successful day c. 1920 when he visited the home of Joseph Cherry in the area that became Tuckahoe State Park. Cherry, his sons, grandchildren, and neighbors posed with the exterminator and his helpers, two ferrets and two rat terriers.

Greensboro's main industry for many years was a large condensed milk plant and an ice cream factory. The town is located near the headwaters of the Choptank River.

Woodburning cook stoves were a specialty of the hardware store at Burrsville c. 1910, below.

Goldsboro grew prosperous when the railroad arrived in 1870 and canneries were established. Later, a truck route went right through the town, so its location continued to be beneficial. Dennison's Store was located on Main Street when the photographs right and below were made c. 1915.

Like many other communities in Maryland, Goldsboro has undergone several name changes. At first it was called Oldtown, but in 1870 it became Goldsborough to honor a local physician who owned much of the land in the surrounding area.

Church Hill, above, takes its name from St. Luke's Protestant Episcopal Church, which cost 140,000 pounds of tobacco to build in 1731.

Mary Semey joined her father and their farm-hands to inspect the livestock at their barn in Price c. 1910. Little Mary grew up to become the keeper of the photographic collection at the Historical Society of Cecil County.

49

Queenstown Landing, far left, was a private wharf on the Chester River. Queenstown was the first seat of government for Queen Anne's County. In 1792 a new courthouse was built in Centreville.

Kent Island was the site of the first English settlement in Maryland in 1631, though the man who established the trading post, William Claiborne, considered his claim to be part of Virginia. This old farmhouse, photographed c. 1875, faced out to the Bay on Still Pond and Church Creek.

This aerial view of Wye Island illustrates the geography of much of the Eastern Shore coast-line: long necks of land cut by rivers and creeks, cultivated to the water's edge. Taken in 1939, the photograph looks west from Skipton Creek.

Love Point's cliffs provide a dramatic illustration of the problem of erosion caused by the Chesapeake Bay. In the century between 1840 and 1940 six thousand acres of land were washed away. As a result, many of the shoulders of the Bay are sandy and the bottom of some channels are covered with clay and silt carried down rivers.

A popular summer resort, Love Point featured a modern hotel, several boarding houses, and bathing facilities. The hotel was a particular favorite with vacationers from Baltimore.

Love Point was the terminus of a ferry line from Baltimore. In 1940 the cost was two dollars for car and driver, additional passengers were fifty cents each.

Love Point is located at the northernmost tip of Kent Island at the mouth of the Chester River.

The waters around the resort were a favorite fishing spot for visiting sportsmen. Many bluefish, rock, and black bass were caught there every year. Love Point was also the end of the line for the Maryland, Delaware and Virginia Railway.

The Canning Season in Maryland

from *The Book of the Royal Blue*, September 1907

Twenty thousand wage-earners more or less are working like Trojans these September days to aid Maryland in maintaining her position of supremacy as the center of America's canning industry.

Of these 20,000 workers more than half are only temporarily employed by the canneries during the rush harvest months; and all of these extra laborers, with an overwhelming majority of the regular canning-house forces, are to-day engaged in packing tomatoes and corn. The vegetable canning season is now in full swing.

In the fields, cutting corn and picking tomatoes; in the packing houses preparing the vegetables and sealing them in tins, and in the warehouses labeling and packing in cases the finished product—this is the work which these many laborers are performing.

The army of workers is made up of men, women and children; and in racial complexion it is a composite of Bohemian, English, German, Ethiopian and, in lesser degree, many other nationalities.

These toilers in the big cities, in the smaller towns and villages, and in the rural sections of Maryland will show as the result of their toil, now just begun in earnest, and which will continue uninterrupted up to the first frost, a total pack of between 3,000,000 and 4,000,000 cases of tomatoes and about one-third as many cases of corn, or an aggregate of something like 100,000,000 cans of the two vegetables.

Wherever seasonal picking jobs were available, migrant workers would make their way to eke out a meager living picking whatever crop was ready for harvest. The camp at left was located in Dorchester County in 1915.

It was not unusual for workers to go out into the fields from 4:00 A.M. until sunset on long, hot, summer days. These bean pickers were photographed by Arthur Rothstein near Cambridge in June 1937.

The larger city packing establishments—frequently housing under one roof several hundred, and even a thousand workers—are, of course, interesting to the outsider, just as any well-regulated manufacturing plant is; but it is rather in the smaller enterprises, scattered broadcast throughout the State, that the average person will find conditions that make the strongest appeal for his attention. The greatest canning establishments lack individuality—each is designedly a well-ordered piece of machinery; while the smaller canneries are all living, emotional creatures with as much personality as a human being.

The cause for this difference is not far to seek. The big city plant is simply a factory. It is in operation all, or nearly all, of the year. It purchases raw material and by commonplace laborers this material is converted into canned goods.

Its employees are in all respects simply factory hands.

On the other hand, the small canning establishments, usually found in the little towns or in a country district near some transportation line, is operated only for a limited season; in the case of vegetable packing houses, only during the harvest season of corn, tomatoes and peas. Its season is short and rapid, for when once the raw material begins to ripen in the field, it matures quickly and simultaneously and must be disposed of before it reaches a stage of decay.

The small rural packer is dependent upon his immediate surrounding territory for his raw material, and therefore the crops available to him all become ready for his use—ready with an urgency—at about the same time, and he who has not been accustomed to running a cannery for almost a year is called upon to direct a plant which enters the field of activity with a spurt and rushes breathlessly through its entire season in a few months.

And, finally the laborers in the majority of out-of-town canneries are imported from the larger cities, and with their crude mode of life while in their temporary quarters they add a bit of fascination to the establishment by which they are employed.

Baltimore has been called the "cradle of the canning industry," and Maryland leads the country in the packing of toma-

Agriculture in Maryland began utilizing scientific approaches toward the end of the nineteenth century. Unfortunately, scale insects grew almost as fast as the fruit in the trees in this Kent County orchard in 1897, necessitating fumigation of the crops.

toes, corn, peas, lima beans and not a few fruits. In the State there are, perhaps, 300 canneries devoted to the packing of vegetables and fruits; the largest, of course, being in the city of Baltimore, but the smaller ones are well distributed through the counties. And there is a tendency today toward the wider distribution of can-

ning energy rather than concentration, which promises well for the farmer who disposes of his product to canners, as well as for the canning industry itself and the material interests of the State.

In sections of Maryland where canning had apparently never before been thought of as an adjunct to the agricultural industry small plants are being erected, and thus there is created a certain market for the truck farmer who heretofore has been dependent upon the rather fickle course of the city produce demand. In many instances, too, there are found under common management or ownership both a canning establishment and a truck farm. Thus a producer

of preservable vegetables enters into the closely allied business of canner, supplying from his own land part of the raw material used by his establishment and also purchasing from his neighbors additional products.

The smaller canneries are usually unpretentious affairs. They are invariably near the source of supply for raw materials, and almost as invariably near a transportation line, although in a few instances canning houses are three and even five miles from their shipping point.

The establishment consists of at least two buildings. One of these—a barnlike structure with one large door, but no windows—is the warehouse where are stored

Millions of tomatoes are grown on the Eastern Shore every year. Ten thousand acres were planted in Dorchester County alone in 1936. When this photograph of a Chester River wharf was made in 1910, most of the crop was processed in county canneries, but part of it was shipped to Baltimore facilities.

By 1940, below, Kent County was exporting most of its tomato crop by truck and boat, with only a small portion being canned locally.

the cases and tins before the packing season begins, and after canning is under way, with the sealed goods, which are subsequently labeled and nailed up in cases.

The other building is the cannery itself. This is, as a rule, a crude structure, open sometimes on one side and sometimes open on two and three, and even all four sides. Here the vegetables are prepared for canning, where they are sealed and

Migrant workers traveled great distances for a few weeks of labor. These pickers from North Carolina were en route from Princess Anne to Easton to harvest beans when the truck transporting them broke down in July 1940. Many of the migrants were children who worked in the fields and canneries keeping virtually the same long hours as their parents.

cooked, and from this building they are generally carted to the nearby warehouse to be labeled and packed in cases, although the cans are sometimes given these finishing touches before they leave the packing room.

To follow in the proper order the business of the canning of vegetables, the first class of laborers encountered is the gatherer of corn from the stalks and the picker of tomatoes from the vine. This work is usually performed by men, as it is both heavy and tiring, and the laborers engaged are as a rule foreign help; that is, they are brought into the section for that particular work, and after it has been performed return again to their homes.

An ordinary establishment in a small town or village might employ three to six pickers, and these are hired from the city. The same men frequently travel in com-

pany, thus being with one another year after year.

The pickers' employment with the cannery lasts anywhere from a few weeks to several months, and during this period they live in a hut in the open field. In one instance five pickers were found living in one tiny building of rough plank, the structure measuring hardly more than eight feet for any one of its three dimensions.

The hut was provided with a door, though no windows, and inside two shelves, about four feet deep and reaching from front to back of the building, served as a pair of double bunks, while the stretch of floor under the lower berth could be utilized as an additional double bed. The bedding had apparently been acquired from a nearby stable. The building overlooked a great tomato field

where the men were to labor, while back of it lay a small clump of trees, under which the duly-appointed mess-cook prepared meals that were neither coarse nor unappetizing.

The tomato picker works hard, but earns fair wages. He is paid at the rate of four cents for gathering a bushel of tomatoes, which does not at first thought seem inviting. This one bushel means the filling twice of the basket that he carries in one hand while going through the patch, and which he empties in the bushel boxes that his employer causes to be strewn along the outskirts of the tomato patch. But the more capable of these pickers can gather in the course of their 10- or 12-hour day anywhere from 75 to 100 bushels of the vegetables, and they frequently work in a good season five and six weeks at a stretch without a break. Despite their humble quarters and their rather heavy labor, the pickers are generally presentable specimens of manhood, and the outing which they enjoy during their season of work in the field is not without its attractive features.

Much the same process followed in the picking of tomatoes is pursued in cutting corn, and the gathered product is placed where it may easily be collected by the cannery wagons and carried off to the packing house.

The laborers in the field who gather the vegetables are more often native Americans than otherwise, but in the cannery proper the foreign element, perhaps, dominates; and here Bohemians and other nationalities are in prominence, and workers of that class, which has as yet imbibed little pertaining to America, are found at the tables. In their labor, in their living quarters and in the atmosphere which surrounds them, there is not found as much to admire as in the cleanly habits of the male vegetable pickers.

The inside cannery employees are also imported as a rule from the cities, and during the several months that they work in the out-of-town packing houses they live in a small settlement somewhere close to the place of their employment. They are, of course, in greater numbers than the pickers, and a moderate-size cannery may employ anywhere from fifteen to fifty workers of this class.

The packers come to the cannery with their entire families, when they have families, and the workers—especially when they are of the same nationality—live in a sort of colony of their own.

Their quarters consist of a collection of rough shanties under a few shade trees, and the various families are crowded into small one-room huts and generally do their cooking in the open in about the same manner as the pickers. The separate

families cook for themselves and do not mess together. Outside of meal hours and sleeping time, however, they freely intermingle with one another.

In the canning of corn, the husks are removed from the ears immediately after the vegetable reaches the cannery. This labor is performed by the less capable women and children, who are paid so much per basket for their work, a full basket being determined by weight.

The rapid increase in the number of canning establishments in Maryland, accompanied by a decrease in the average capital per establishment and the average number of employees, indicates a healthy growth of the canning industry in smaller establishments. This increase is largely noticeable in the heart of farming districts and, as has already been noted, means a great benefit to the agricultural class.

In addition to the certain market which a cannery establishes for the nearby

Conditions like these at the Phillips Packing Company in Vienna were typical of living quarters provided for migrant workers.

farmers for their truck produce, there comes from it, as a by-product, the slops, which have a very considerable market value as feed.

No matter how thin and frisky the pig population near a cannery may be before the opening of the canning season, it is sure to be transformed by the close of the season, through the agency of corn husks and cobs and tomato waste, into a race of fat and lazy swine.

Even the canner himself in a prosperous season cannot take on more flesh than this parasite at the end of the waste-pipe of his factory, and the refuse of a canning season finds itself by fall converted into many pounds of bacon and ham.

The Reed Rifles, right, were a local militia organized in 1858 in Chestertown. They were called out several times to quell disorders when excursionists from Baltimore became rowdy. The group disbanded at the outbreak of the Civil War and most members enlisted in the Home Guard, which was encamped at a mill near Chestertown.

Chestertown, the seat of Kent County, was first settled as New Town by 1698 when the courthouse was built. The current name was assumed in 1780 when the charter was revised. The view below was made from across the Chester River on the Queen Anne's County side. Chestertown is the home of Washington College. Founded in 1782, it was the first college to adopt the name of George Washington.

George H. Risgle, sixty-three years old, had been selling oysters for thirty-eight years in Chestertown at the time this photograph was made in 1940.

FOLLOWING PAGES:
Steamships were a primary form of transportation between 1840 and 1940, especially on the Eastern Shore and in Southern Maryland. The Louise, *photographed on the Bay in 1912, carried thousands of happy excursionists from Baltimore to Tolchester Beach resort.*

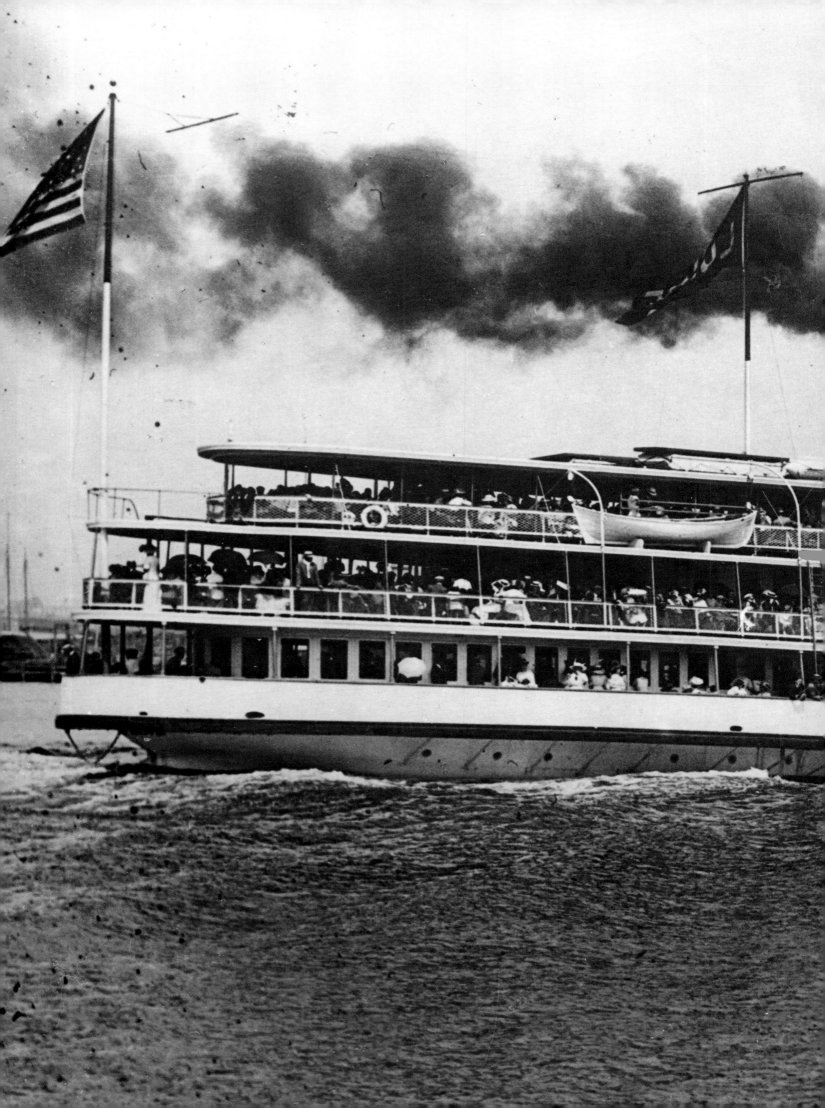

Tolchester Beach, opened in 1877, was a mecca for day-trippers from all over Maryland. Steamboats from Baltimore arrived twice daily (at a fee of two dollars per car and driver in 1940) to deliver thousands of merrymakers for a day of fun and frolicking at the amusement park.

Photographer Henry Rinn, Jr., was a frequent visitor to Chesapeake Bay resorts and made quite a business of publishing picture post cards of views he made at Tolchester and Betterton beaches. The scenes on these and the following pages were printed from his original glass-plate negatives made c. 1905.

Betterton Beach is located at the mouth of the Sassafras River in northern Kent County. Its excellent beach and hotels made it a favorite vacation spot for many, especially Baltimoreans.

The sign on the tent with its flaps opened (in the center of the photograph below) invites bathers into a postal-card photo gallery. The first decade of the twentieth century was the heyday of the picture post card. Some were original photographic prints, and hundreds of these have survived. In a few cases they are the only visual record of a community during that period.

The sign was altered and the building painted but little else changed between the times these photographs of the Chesapeake House Hotel, below and far right, were made by Henry Rinn, Jr.

In spite of its name, Sassafras is not located on the Sassafras River, though it is near the river's headwaters. Captain John Smith, who first explored the river, named it the Tockwough after the tribe of Indians who inhabited its banks. Tockwough is the original Indian word for sassafras. Dreka Mill, right, was located near the village of Sassafras.

The house at Dreka Mill featured unusually ornate ironwork on its front porch. This photograph was made c. 1885.

There are eight places in Maryland named Town Point. Cecil County has two: one, the actual point of land projecting into the Elk River, was the location of this photograph of a boating party in 1909. The other is the village of Town Point, about two miles inland between the Elk and the Bohemia rivers.

Chesapeake City, below, is the Maryland terminus of the Chesapeake & Delaware Canal. The town owes its existence to the opening of the waterway in 1829. It cut the distance between Baltimore and Philadelphia by 286 miles—at an original cost of $2,200,000. The federal government removed the locks and lowered the canal to sea level in 1927, making it possible for all but the largest ocean liners and battleships to navigate the distance between the Delaware and Chesapeake bays.

Elkton, the seat of Cecil County, was the hometown of Company I of the Fifth Maryland Volunteers during the Civil War. The tintype at right, made in 1862, shows a number of covered wagons behind the soldiers. One bears a sign that reads "No. 11 Supper Train."

Elkton is located on the Elk River, virtually at the top of the Chesapeake Bay. It has been an important port since before the Revolution, and in 1807 it was a primary American wheat market, handling 250,000 bushels a year. Elkton was home to the Scott Fertilizer Company, whose building is seen below on the right, as well as to manufacturers of paper, pulp, flour, and shirts in 1940.

Until 1938, Elkton's biggest industry was marriage. Because Maryland required no waiting time after a marriage license was obtained, many couples eloping from New York and beyond stopped in Elkton—the first big town over the state line—to tie the knot. Finally, the legislature became outraged by the notoriety the town was achieving and put a halt to the practice by passing a law requiring a forty-eight-hour waiting period.

There wasn't much of a crowd for this parade on Main Street c. 1919. Perhaps there was a better turnout for Lafayette's troops as they embarked from Elkton to Annapolis in March 1781, or for Washington, when he and his army passed through on their way to Yorktown later that year.

Charlestown was the seat of Cecil County until the courthouse was moved to Elkton in 1786. Located on the Northeast River at the head of the Chesapeake Bay, Charlestown was the site of several popular beaches. Murphy's, photographed at right in 1939, rented canoes and rowboats.

Holloway Beach, below, apparently was the more popular of the two swimming spots c. 1940.

It was quite an event when the railroad bridge over Principio Creek collapsed on the Philadelphia, Baltimore and Washington line in 1904. It took a bit of time, but the engine was finally lifted by two cranes back onto the tracks of the repaired bridge.

73

Perryville, located at the mouth of the Susquehanna River, was the site of this reunion of Snow's Battery, right. The Civil War veterans, meeting twenty years later, got out their medals for the occasion.

The students at Perryville Public School on Susquehanna Avenue made a big effort to appear studious for their class portrait. Their teacher, seated at the table at the center, apparently succeeded in instilling his charges with a love for books.

Employees at the Armstrong Stove Foundry in Perryville didn't bother to wash their faces for the camera.

Rising Sun, just two miles from the Pennsylvania border, took its name in 1816 from a local tavern that had a picture of a sun peeping over the horizon on its sign. Students at the local public high school posed for the portrait above c. 1915.

Long after slavery was abolished, Maryland blacks were permitted for the most part to work only at manual labor. As a result, their homes were rarely more comfortable than this old log cabin in Cecil County.

75

Religious revival camps were an annual summer ritual for many Marylanders. Woodlawn Camp in Cecil County was a popular meeting place for Methodists c. 1896. White, of course, was the fashionable color for young women at Woodlawn Camp.

Before the construction of the Conowingo Dam in 1927, the Susquehanna River would regularly be backed up by enormous ice gorges in the winter. The one pictured at left and far below, c. 1904, caused floes that piled up more than ten feet when a path was cut through.

At one time the granite quarry at Port Deposit, above, employed several hundred people. Many buildings in the town were constructed of granite.

Port Deposit, six miles from the mouth of the Susquehanna, occasionally suffered damage from the ice gorges. The Tome Memorial Church, seen in the distance at left, was named to honor the town's greatest benefactor, the self-made millionaire who ran a lumber business here for many years. He is remembered for financing the Tome School, a boys' boarding school opened in 1900 in Port Deposit.

CENTRAL Maryland

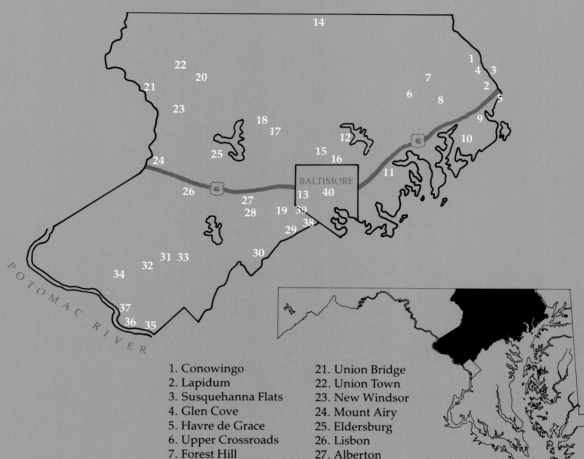

1. Conowingo
2. Lapidum
3. Susquehanna Flats
4. Glen Cove
5. Havre de Grace
6. Upper Crossroads
7. Forest Hill
8. Bel Air
9. Aberdeen
10. Perryman
11. White Marsh
12. Loch Raven Dam
13. Gwynn's Falls
14. Freeland
15. Timonium
16. Towson
17. Glyndon
18. Reisterstown
19. Catonsville
20. Westminster

21. Union Bridge
22. Union Town
23. New Windsor
24. Mount Airy
25. Eldersburg
26. Lisbon
27. Alberton
28. Ellicott City
29. Elkridge
30. Savage Station
31. Olney
32. Washington Grove
33. Sandy Spring
34. Rockville
35. Glen Echo*
36. Cabin John Bridge*
37. Great Falls*
38. Relay
39. Halethorpe
40. Baltimore

*On the C & O Canal

From the beginning of the twentieth century, suburbia began to dominate much of Central Maryland. This house in Sudbrook, a planned community in Baltimore, was the home of the Merrick family, pictured here in 1898. The charming young gentleman dressed in white is Robert G. Merrick, who grew up to become one of the city's premier financiers and most benevolent philanthropists.

The Susquehanna River divides not only Cecil and Harford counties but is also a natural border separating the Maryland mainland from the Eastern Shore. The village of Conowingo, right, was at one time the site of a lock on the Susquehanna and Tidewater Canal, which opened in 1839. Barges drawn by mules made their way up the canal to Wrightsville, Pennsylvania, a forty-five mile run. Conowingo lent its name to nearby Conowingo Dam, completed in 1927. Less than a mile long and one-hundred-feet high, the dam provides electrical power to several states.

The Susquehanna and Tidewater Canal, seen below at Lapidum, was once part of a viable shipping route between Baltimore and Philadelphia. Waterways were never able to compete successfully with railroads, however. By 1900 this canal was a relic.

The Susquehanna flows 444 miles, from central New York State through Pennsylvania to the head of the Chesapeake Bay, but it is navigable for only 5 miles.

Fishing has long been a profitable enterprise for those living along the shores of the river. The crews pictured left and below were working just above Havre de Grace in 1899.

Samuel and Sarah White and their fourteen children lived in this modest cottage in Glen Cove, c. 1925.

The Baltimore & Ohio Railroad bridge across the
Susquehanna River was converted from a wooden
to a steel structure from 1873 to 1879. The job
was apparently completed when this photograph
was made.

The lock keeper's house at Havre de Grace fell
into severe disrepair after the closing of the Susquehanna and Tidewater Canal. An ice gorge
on the river was in progress at the time the picture at right was made. In recent years the
house has been restored and transformed into a
museum.

Public schools like the one at Upper Crossroads, c. 1912, left, came into being as a result of the creation of a State Board of Education in 1864. Prior to that time schools were a low priority in many communities, and attendance was not required.

Priest Neale's Mass House, above, was built c. 1750 as the home of the first Jesuit priests in Harford County. It was July 4, 1888, when this family group posed in front of the landmark, which still stands on Cool Spring Road between Churchville and Dublin.

Forest Hill, left, was located on the Maryland and Pennsylvania Railroad. Although this postcard view was made c. 1910, no automobiles were in evidence.

Hanway Brothers' store on the northeast corner of Main Street and Churchville Road in Bel Air specialized in hardware and farm implements. As the county seat, the town became a trading center for the surrounding countryside. Hunting and horse breeding and racing are all time-honored traditions in fertile Harford County.

Governor Edwin Warfield rode into Bel Air c. 1904 to review an encampment of the entire Maryland National Guard.

Although Aberdeen has gained its greatest notoriety as the location of the federal government's testing grounds for ordnance, shells, bombs, mines, and other military materiel, the town existed well before the Proving Grounds came into being. The sleepy scene at left shows Broadway, one of Aberdeen's main streets, c. 1910.

The citizens of Bel Air turned out in large numbers to greet Company D of the National Guard when it arrived at the Maryland and Pennsylvania Railroad Station after summer camp, c. 1905.

Bel Air was not incorporated until 1901, although it had been the county seat since 1782, when it was called Aquila Scott's Old Field. The general appearance of the town has remained remarkably unchanged since the 1933 view at left was made.

85

Commuter trains still stop at the Perryman Station, adjacent to the Aberdeen Proving Grounds.

Smith's Hall was located in Chase, a small town in Baltimore County. The area has remained a profitable one for merchants: nearby White Marsh was developed into a shopping center seventy years later.

This early stereographic view, probably made c. 1870, was titled simply, "The Village Blacksmith, near Baltimore."

The original Loch Raven Dam, seen at left while still under construction in 1881, supplied Baltimore City with water. Its source was the Gunpowder River. The opening of the system was celebrated in October 1881 with a gala affair called the Baltimore Oriole which attracted 150,000 visitors.

Henry Rinn, Jr., photographed his wife and son strolling beside Gwynn's Falls c. 1905, just a few years after the city appropriated funds for a twenty-eight–acre park there. Little Henry wore the same straw hat in many of his father's picture post-card views made in and around Baltimore.

The rich farmland of Baltimore County once attracted many migrant workers during the picking season. Little Annie Bissie posed for photographer Lewis Hine in July 1909.

An 1881 geography textbook described Baltimore County as ''the richest and most populous county of Maryland. The surface is in some parts undulating, and in others broken by bold hills. Agriculture is skillfully conducted, and the farmer is rewarded with large crops of grain, potatoes, and hay, and an abundance of garden and dairy products.'' It is also a large county, extending from the Patapsco River to the Pennsylvania border. Freeland, pictured below c. 1910, is just two miles from the state line.

This Polish family pictured near Baltimore in July 1909 had harvested crops in Biloxi, Mississippi, the previous two years.

The Maryland State Fair begins on Labor Day every year in Timonium. At right, a future farmer showed off his prize sheep on September 15, 1933.

Later that same day, the family below was intrigued by a photographer's rather odd-looking camera. The apparatus was probably part of an instantaneous wet process technique that was popular about that time.

The midway at Timonium was crowded on opening day in 1936.

Although primarily an agricultural event, the state fair draws people from all walks of life to the amusements and entertainment, which are an integral part of each fair.

More than half of the midway strollers in 1940, left and below, were wearing hats, many of which were probably manufactured in Baltimore.

Towson has been the seat of Baltimore County government since 1854, when the separation of the city and county was finalized. In 1906 the St. Denis Volunteer Fire Department journeyed there for a statewide association meeting.

Towson remained a quiet little town for many years, as evidenced in the picture of Lee's Corner c. 1912, below. Gradually, though, because of its location Towson lost some of its own identity and by 1940 it was essentially a suburb of the city of Baltimore.

On Memorial Day in 1936 soldiers, sailors, and civilians gathered to pay tribute at the War Memorial in Towson. A few years later Hutzlers' Department Store opened a branch just up the street.

92

The Western Maryland Railway station at Glyndon served as a commuter station for only a few years c. 1904. Later, the building was converted into a post office.

The village of Glyndon is less than a mile from Reisterstown. By 1940, 490 persons lived along its neat, tree-lined streets.

Reisterstown was settled by John Reister, a German immigrant, and his family in 1758. Its strategic location on the road to Gettysburg and Hanover, Pennsylvania, occasioned the establishment of several excellent inns and taverns in Reisterstown.

Franklin Academy, right and below, was opened in 1820 as a private school. In 1897 it became Baltimore County's first public high school; students and teachers who attended Franklin at the turn of the century are pictured here. It is reported that Edgar Allan Poe once applied for the position of principal at the academy but was turned down.

Home economics students at Franklin High School, c. 1900, appear captivated by a cooking demonstration on eggs.

The 1926 graduating class of Hannah More Academy, left, was part of a proud tradition of outstanding young women who had attended the school since its founding in 1832. In 1873 Hannah More became a diocesan school of the Protestant Episcopal Church. Baltimore County enjoys a plethora of excellent educational institutions located within its boundaries.

The West Point Sunday School was apparently a very serious group c. 1910, below.

Baltimore County has a well-deserved reputation for foxhunting and horse breeding and racing. Miss Sarah Bell Williams, right, was a charming member of the horsey set and of Baltimore society. She later made her home in Annapolis. Note the side saddle.

Colonel Edward Morrel drove his four-in-hand to the Devon Horse Show in May 1890 with Fanny Lurman as his guest.

Catonsville is older than the city of Baltimore. First called Johnnycake, it was renamed about 1800 to honor Richard Caton, a son-in-law of Charles Carroll of Carrollton, who owned an estate there. C. F. Wise's saloon was located at the corner of Edmondson Road and Ingleside Avenue before 1900.

Mr. Peregoy kept his grocery store at 833 Frederick Road well supplied with cookies, comfortably within reach from his roll-top desk.

F. A. Seicke, Jr., offered all sorts of services at his store at 715 Frederick Road in Catonsville, left. Telephones, sign painting, burglar alarms, electric and gas lighting were all featured at Seicke's in 1895.

FOLLOWING PAGES:
The charm of this May Day celebration disguises the fact that the participants were patients at the Spring Grove State Hospital. There were few such pleasant facilities for the mentally ill in the nineteenth century. For the most part, the poor and the insane co-mingled with little supervision or care in county almshouses.

Westminster is the seat of Carroll County. The view of Main Street looking west from Bond Street, right, was made c. 1861, the same year the Western Maryland Railway came to town. Two years later, on June 28, 1863, Confederate troops raided Westminster. The next day the entire Union army passed through on the way to Gettysburg.

Western Maryland College was founded as a private academy in 1860; it was reorganized as a college under the supervision of the Methodist Church in 1866. The 1888 view below looks back over Westminster from the campus located on the northwestern outskirts of town.

The Guide to the Old Line State *describes Westminster as "a prosperous, conservative community of neat homes where neither affluence nor poverty are apparent and where the village banker may live next door to the carpenter or the local lawyer may have the barber for a neighbor." Westminster, of course, was the trading center for the surrounding area. Smith & Reifsnider's apparently did a brisk business c. 1885 when the photograph above was made.*

Miss Lottie Owings practiced her teaching skills in a classroom at Western Maryland College in 1888.

Far left, Theodore Roosevelt struck an uncharacteristically somber pose as he prepared to give a speech in Westminster during the presidential campaign of 1912. Roosevelt was the guest of American Sentinel *editor Joseph L. Brooks, who introduced him to an enthusiastic crowd.*

Carroll County, named for Charles Carroll of Carrollton, was carved out of parts of Baltimore and Frederick counties in 1837. Covered wagons like the one pictured at left in Carroll County c. 1856 were first built in Conestoga, Pennsylvania—hence the appellation, Conestoga wagon.

The Reifsniders brought out all the members of their household for a family portrait c. 1885. Their home, a villa they called Terrace Hill, later became part of the Western Maryland College campus.

Union Bridge was settled on Little Pipe Creek in the 1730s. Home of the first nail factory in the United States, the town has a proud tradition of industrial production. A parade in 1897 inspired this float representing the Western Maryland Railway machine shop located in Union Bridge. The tower atop the display symbolizes the observatory at Pen Mar Park, a mountain resort operated by the Western Maryland Railway.

William Henry Rinehart, the famous sculptor, was born in this Carroll County house near Union Bridge in 1825. Rinehart's father owned a local quarry. The sculptor learned stone cutting in Baltimore and attended classes at the Maryland Institute of Art in Baltimore. His work has been exhibited in major museums throughout the world. Note the ancient black woman at the right who probably lived part of her life in slavery.

Romance appears to have been on the minds of these young people from Uniontown c. 1890.

Little Pipe Creek forms part of the border between Carroll and Frederick counties. This Pennsylvania Railroad train chugged across the Little Pipe Creek trestle bridge c. 1900.

New Windsor was called Sulphur Springs when it was first settled in the early nineteenth century. Dielman's Inn, right, was a popular stopping point on the road to Frederick.

Cement was being laid on the New Windsor Road in front of the Wakefield Valley Church when the photograph below was made c. 1920.

Mount Airy is located on the border of Carroll and Frederick counties. The local drugstore had a generous supply of pharmaceuticals stocked on its shelves.

Robert Strawbridge introduced Methodism to the United States in Carroll County in about 1764. His style of preaching without a book or manuscript was considered revolutionary at the time. The Strawbridge Methodist Pilgrimmage, above, was named in his honor.

Mr. Barnes believed in advertising his merchandise at this Mount Airy furniture store c. 1905, left.

Howard County, named for Maryland's famed Revolutionary War hero John Eager Howard, was created from parts of Anne Arundel and Baltimore counties in 1851. "Lynnwood," right, was the estate home of James C. Adams, Sr. Until rerouting of the highway passed it by, the home was for a time used as a restaurant.

The National Road passed through the middle of the village of Lisbon, pictured below in August 1912.

The Gary School, left, c. 1905, was located in Alberton, near Ellicott City. When the mill at Alberton went bankrupt in 1941 the entire town was sold for $65,000.

On May 24, 1830, the first railroad—drawn by horses—in the United States arrived in Ellicott City from Baltimore, thirteen miles away. The Baltimore & Ohio station pictured above c. 1905 was in continuous use for many years until it was converted into a museum.

Ellicott City is the seat of Howard County government and its principal banking and trading center. Winding Main Street follows a narrow ravine, and some buildings on the south side are constructed over the Tiber Creek. Many of the older homes and stores are made of local granite.

109

John, Joseph, and Andrew Ellicott first bought the land and water rights for what became Ellicott City in 1774. They brought machinery of their own invention and harnessed the power of the Patapsco River to operate grist and flour mills.

Samuel W. Burgess maintained a grist mill and wagon works on Tiber Creek in Ellicott City from 1906 to 1917, left and far left. The view on the opposite page illustrates the housing of the water wheel and an aqueduct that carried water across Tiber Creek from the mill race.

The Ellicott family operated the Patapsco Flour Mill, below, for sixty years. In 1837 it was taken over by Charles Gambrill and Charles Carroll (son of Charles Carroll of Carrollton).

Although only one Civil War battle was fought on Maryland soil, war-related activities were carried on throughout the state all during the conflict. At right, wounded soldiers were transported on the Baltimore & Ohio Railroad to Savage Station after the battle of June 27, 1862. There they were photographed in all their pain and misery by James F. Gibson.

Below, the cook house of Company A of the Eighth Massachusetts Infantry posed at Elkridge Heights on June 13, 1861.

In 1884 the Hanson family, above, owned Belmont, a five-part, two-story brick house originally built by Caleb Dorsey in 1738. Dorsey owned nearby iron mines. By 1940 the boxwood hedge surrounding the house was fifteen-feet high in some places.

The Patapsco River was once navigable all the way to Elkridge, and before the Revolution the town rivaled Annapolis as the leading port of the province. During the war, forges and furnaces produced arms for the Continental army. At left, horseback riders admire the Olney estate near Elkridge, c. 1885.

113

Although Montgomery County was created in 1776 there was not a single town within its borders until Rockville was developed after 1804. The laying of the cornerstone for Montgomery General Hospital in Olney attracted a small crowd c. 1918, right.

In the twentieth century much of Montgomery County evolved into suburban developments for federal workers from Washington, D.C. Towns like Olney, above, once dotted the countryside; in later years the area became so populous that it became difficult to distinguish one community from the next.

The ladies of Washington Grove (near Gaithersburg) met at the Woman's Club in 1910, right.

Sandy Spring is the oldest settlement in the county, established by Quakers in 1650. It remained a popular meeting place for the Friends, including the Quaker ladies at left.

Rockville has been the county seat of Montgomery County since 1777, although it was first called Montgomery Court House, and later Williamsburg. The classic picture post-card view of the Triangle, below, was made c. 1910.

Vinson's Store on East Montgomery Avenue, far below, was owned by D. E. Owens and operated as a drugstore. Vinson took over the establishment c. 1910.

FOLLOWING PAGES:
The Chesapeake & Ohio Canal was begun in Georgetown on July 4, 1828—the very same day that the cornerstone of the Baltimore & Ohio Railroad was laid in Baltimore. Canal and railroad competed for land rights: both wanted to follow the path of the Potomac River to Cumberland, 187 miles away, and in some places the passage was too narrow for waterway and rail line. Serious financial problems delayed the completion of the canal to Cumberland until 1850—eight years after the railroad reached that point. This photograph depicts the Glen Echo Lock, the eighth of a total of seventy-four locks on the canal which raised it from sea level at Georgetown to 610 feet in Cumberland.

115

The Cabin John Bridge was begun in 1857 and completed in 1864. Jefferson Davis was secretary of war when it was started, but his name was removed from a plaque on the bridge when he became president of the Confederacy. It was restored during Theodore Roosevelt's administration. The photograph at right shows the condition of the bridge in 1859.

At the time the Cabin John Bridge was constructed it was the largest single-arch span in the Western Hemisphere, 220 feet in length. The view below was made in 1900.

118

This camper was about to enjoy a hearty meal cooked along the banks of the Potomac River.

The viaduct at Great Falls was still under construction when the photograph below was made on May 10, 1858.

The solitary fisherman found a quiet spot along the Potomac, c. 1906.

The Sixth Massachusetts Regiment formed part of the guard stationed at Relay House, above, in May 1861. The troops attempted to stop Baltimore's generous supply of recruits and materials to the Confederate army at Harpers Ferry, and they stood ready to squelch any attempt by the Confederates to move toward Relay.

The Thomas Viaduct transports the Baltimore & Ohio Railroad across the Patapsco River between Relay and Elkridge. Constructed in 1835 of granite formed into eight elliptical arches, the structure forms a graceful curve 612 feet long. In May 1861 General Benjamin Butler and his troops occupied Relay. Two guns were planted on the hill overlooking the bridge.

Relay got its name in the early days of railroading when power for trains was furnished by horses. At this location there was a station where relays of horses were kept to continue the movement of trains the six additional miles to Ellicott City, the end of the line at the time.

120

Halethorpe, in Baltimore County just southwest of the city, was the site of the Fair of the Iron Horse, an extravaganza celebrating the centennial of the Baltimore & Ohio Railroad, in September 1927. The primary theme of the many exhibitions was transportation in all its forms from stagecoaches to armored trucks, but the main emphasis was on railroads.

The event attracted more than 1,250,000 people. One of the highlights was a settlement of Blackfoot Indians from Glacier National Park.

Many of the exhibits viewed by the enormous crowds in the grandstand at the Fair of the Iron Horse were later displayed at the Baltimore & Ohio Transportation Museum at Mount Clare Station in Baltimore.

Lower left, an executive of the Baltimore Gas and Electric Company was on hand to greet some of the Blackfoot Indian participants in the Fair.

No fair would be complete without a midway. The concessions at the Fair of the Iron Horse, lower right, did a brisk business.

123

Baltimore achieved the position of Maryland's leading city primarily because of its strategic location. The wide estuary of the Patapsco River formed a large sheltered harbor, and nearby streams provided water power for industries. When Camden Station, above, was built in 1852 it was the largest railroad station in the world.

The US Constellation was launched from Baltimore in 1797. It is the oldest sailing vessel to have served in the U.S. Navy during wartime.

The inner harbor at Pratt Street has always been the scene of busy maritime activities, far right. The street was named in honor of Charles Pratt, the first earl of Camden, an English statesman who supported the colonists in the Revolution.

America's Largest Immigrant Pier

BY GEORGE B. LUCKEY

from *The Book of the Royal Blue*, July 1904

*H*as she reported yet? is the query at the big pier, and if the answer is yes, you know the ship is past in the Capes and the hour of her arrival is practically as certain as that of a railroad train. How many does she bring? is heard from all sides, and upon the answer depends the activity of the morrow. For in the vernacular of the pier this applies to the number of immigrants on board the ship. Here all seems to go by quantity; there are no long lists of social celebrities, no famous actresses, musicians or foreign notables; it is a question of units, each unit representing a hundred people. Quietly the preliminary arrangements are made for the reception of the ship in the morning, while the thousand or two souls—prospective American citizens— pass quietly up the Bay, and in the early morn get their first glimpse of Baltimore and its harbor, as the ship is warped slowly into her dock. The long ocean trip is ended and the great unknown is before them. For one long day this wharf is to be to them all they will see of the land which probably has been a dream of the past. The fantasy of freedom and obscure mirage of the horn of plenty, all too soon to be shadowed into the grim reality of congested mankind; struggling, pushing, even as they have pushed in the land they have just left.

When one thinks of immigration it is a natural impulse to at once think of New York. From this port emanate all the stories of immigration, till it has almost

Huge numbers of immigrants first touched American soil on Locust Point where the Baltimore & Ohio Railroad operated the largest immigration facility in the country in 1904. The new arrivals, at left, started their long journey in Breman, Germany.

Signs at the lunch counter on the immigrant pier were in various languages, and foods familiar to the newcomers were served along with American standards. Soft drinks were particularly popular.

become second nature to look upon Ellis Island as the only inlet into the United States. Instinctively one sees the statue of Liberty with her flaming torch welcoming the loaded liner to port, and the immense bulwark of Manhattan in the background; yet far to the southward, at Baltimore, annually come thousands of these seekers after new homes. This year is an epoch in the history of immigration to this port, for it marks the completion of a new pier by the Baltimore & Ohio Railroad, designed and built expressly for the handling of this class of business.

The first glimpse from the dock of an arriving ship is bewildering in its vast bulk of people, packed closely together. It

seems impossible that so many could find sleeping accommodations, for the immensity of the ship is lost sight of. Great bundles of baggage everywhere on the deck serve as seats, and around and through all are the children, a constant moving, shifting kaleidoscope of color.

Some line the rail and look with wondering eyes at their new strange surroundings, while others stand and sit in stolid indifference. One misses the cries of welcome, the frantic waving of handkerchiefs and the delight in the faces of natives returning to their own shores. Now and then can be picked out a joyous face of welcome from among the few who have friends on the pier, but as a whole there are none to welcome, no cries of recognition; the silence is strange and oppressive, for to the vast majority it is only the beginning of the end. The long companionways are quickly lowered to the deck and the real business of the day commences. Frantic search is made for lost children, innumerable bundles are collected (for the immigrant takes kindly to bundles) and all crowd forward with one impulse, seemingly desirous to be the first to land, and apparently fearful of being left behind. The women are landed first. They come up the gang plank with great bundles balanced on their heads, their babies clasped tightly in their arms and the older children clinging to their skirts. Even these children are burden-bearers, the loads in many cases apparently far too heavy for their puny strength. Stumbling, pushing, but finally triumphant, they land on the dock with all their possessions in tow. Then come the men, who during the interval have been patiently waiting the command to land. The same crowding at the gang plank, the same pushing and frantic haste, more bundles, boxes and even bales, and finally the ship has been unloaded. Here Uncle Sam takes complete charge, and the immigrant suddenly finds himself enmeshed in the red tape net of the Government. The pier now rapidly takes on the appearance of a foreign land. With Aladdin-like swiftness, one has been suddenly deported. They bear still the characteristics they brought away with them; the strange costumes, mannerisms and languages. Long comfortable benches are scattered throughout the big room, into which they are first landed, and these are quickly filled. Hundreds take advantage of every window or door-way to obtain a further look at the harbor, and even the land side comes in for a close scrutiny. After a brief period a portion of the big crowd are taken through a door-way into the main hall where are located the separating pens.

A complete list of all the immigrants has reached the custom and immigration officials, generally by way of New York on a faster steamer and from there mailed to Baltimore. The names have been grouped, each group being lettered. They are soon subdivided and the different letters arranged in the pens. As they pass into this portion of the pier the doctors make their preliminary inspections. Each immigrant in turn being halted and closely scrutinized. The principal disease sought after by the medical staff is trachoma, a contagious disease of the eye. The eyelids are dexterously lifted up by the doctors, as this disease usually lurks

under the lids. A glance is sufficient. Then the head and scalp are looked over for sores denoting any contagious disease, and the entire physical condition is seen at a glance. If there are any suspicious signs apparent to the doctor, the applicant for admission is quickly separated and held in a separate room for special medical examination. The great mass of the immigrants pass the examination of the doctors in a moment. Health seems their common lot. Strong bodies they at least bring over here.

For many years German and Irish immigrants formed a majority, but by the turn of the century they were joined by Poles, Italians, Scandinavians, Czechs, Lithuanians, Greeks, and Russians in large numbers.

Immigrants were not permitted to bring much baggage, so their few worldly possessions were considered great treasures as they arrived in a strange land.

The women particularly have the broad shoulders and hips, denoting almost, if not equal strength of a man. All contagious diseases which can be cured by proper attention are sent to hospitals, where the patients are held under Government orders till cured, then they are allowed to proceed to their destination. A few recognized incurable diseases are entirely debarred, and the poor unfortunate coming under these classes is quickly sent back to his native land.

After passing the inspectors the next move is to obtain their railroad ticket. In the case where the advice sheet has come by a faster steamer to New York, these tickets are ready for distribution upon presentation of their order. Generally the immigrant has purchased his ticket upon the other side directly to his destination and is given an order on the agent here for the railroad portion. In some cases friends on this side have purchased their tickets and they are ready upon demand.

The immigrants seem to have a dread of being parted, even for a moment, from their baggage, and in all their movements lug with them all their belongings; it seems the one tangible link which binds them to their own country, and necessarily impedes the handling of the situation as a whole by the officials. With his railroad ticket finally in his possession, his next thought is to have his money changed into U.S. currency. A booth is maintained here for this purpose and the values printed on a board in different languages is prominently displayed for his guidance.

They carefully count the amount handed them in return for the money of their own country; they rarely seem in doubt as to the correctness of the amount. They will detect a shortage immediately, but there yet remains a case where a surplus has been returned. They are now ready for the inspection of their baggage, which by this time has reached a period of rest.

Many heated altercations take place over the re-packing and a loss of temper is never noticed; the services of the interpreter are not required. The apparently impossible is actually accomplished at last and the baggage is checked at the baggage room to its destination. In most cases the baggage is far in excess of weight carried on the ticket, and has to be weighed and the difference paid for, previous to checking. After all has been straightened out, bales and hampers (for very few trunks are used) are ready for the train, and at last pass out of the eternal vigilance of their owners.

Now comes a wait for the train, as the immigrants are not allowed to leave the pier until they pass directly to their cars. This is the social period, conversation

breaks out and life is again worth the living. At noon time great baskets of bread and meat are brought from the ship to the pier and at once commences a wild scramble for food. Fingers take the place of knives and forks and the bread and meat is eagerly devoured. The steamship companies are responsible for their maintenance till they take the train. An excellent lunch counter is a feature of the pier,

and here can be obtained all the homely foods they are accustomed to, and many delicacies besides. Vast quantities of soft drinks are consumed, but foods new to them are approached with caution, and only purchased by the most adventurous. Many of the immigrants are musical. Accordions are requisitioned and the songs of their native land are played. Sometimes a group of Swiss mountaineers will break into the peculiar yodel songs of their native hills and peasant women sing their babies to sleep with the folk song of their country.

Many marriages take place on the pier, for the law demands that single girls coming to their fiances shall be married before they can land. These marriages form pleasant breaks in the day and the bride is congratulated on all sides. There are several ministers constantly in attendance for this purpose. The costumes of the immigrants of the present day are not nearly as picturesque as those worn

Before the new immigrant pier seen in the previous photographs was completed in 1904, most of the new arrivals landed at the Baltimore & Ohio Railroad piers built c. 1872. Trains backed right up to the building and most passengers headed for points west without ever really seeing Baltimore. As ships grew larger the facility became inadequate.

eighteen or twenty years ago. The wooden shoes of the lowlands of Germany are never seen now, and it is difficult to guess their nationality from their

Immigrants were separated alphabetically into holding pens to await inspection by doctors.

dress alone. The total absence of hats is conspicuous, for the women all wear handkerchiefs, generally of gaudy colors and often of silk. Now and then can be seen short skirts and boots to the knees, but the majority have no striking mode of dress. It is their faces, their gestures and their talk that go to make the picture, as a whole, so interesting. There are several missionaries stationed at the pier who help the immigrants in many ways; they give out booklets containing good advice, and instructions for their best welfare. They refer them, if they are interested, to the minister in the town to which they are going, who in turn helps them to find homes and employment. An interesting point on the pier is the pen into which finally come all those who will remain in Baltimore. A big door gives access to the public portion of the pier, a wooden grating holding back the anxious friends and relatives. Here can be seen the one touch of real enthusiasm and human interest. Frantic greetings of endearment are shouted through the door-way and all is pandemonium. A card comes direct from the inspector with each immigrant and the stories of those claiming their own must tally in every particular with the cards. It seems to the uninitiated that order will never come from such chaos, but it does, and one after another they are claimed and led away by their happy friends and relatives.

On July 24, 1868, a record flood washed out most of the bridges along Jones Falls, including the Gay Street Bridge, far left. It rained seven inches in twenty-four hours, filling two thousand cellars to their ceilings. As a result, plans were finally made to divert the Falls into a tunnel and a canal to Back River.

Baltimore has long been famous for its markets, both those in large buildings like Lexington and Marsh and those in open-air street stalls. The Wholesale Fish Market, seen at left in 1896, supplied restaurants and homemakers alike with much of the fresh seafood that gave the city a glowing reputation for its cuisine.

Farmers from far and wide delivered their produce by truck and boat and set up business in the streets in front of the Fish Market in 1928, below.

Public transportation in Baltimore took the shape of omnibuses like the one at right until 1859 when a new system of horse-drawn streetcars was inaugurated. At that time a tax was levied on the streetcar companies to help finance the city's beautification program. A penny tax on a five-cent fare provided funds for Druid Lake, parks, and plantings along many of the city's boulevards and avenues.

Streetcar lines extended into the suburbs in virtually every direction affording city dwellers easy access to open spaces.

Street Car Chivalry

BY A. R. McCOY

from *Stray Thoughts*, 1876

We suppose that few who have traveled much in the several sections of the Union have failed to notice the street car manners of their fellow travelers. Take the Eastern and Middle States. When Mr. Busy-brain enters a rail or street car he takes a seat if he can crowd into one, and he keeps it, notwithstanding the many females that stand not-expectant around him. This has been customary as many years back as our memory goes. In Maryland and the other Southern States some

years ago, this was entirely different. It was part of "Woman's Rights" always to have the preference in a seat. No matter how much business was to be talked with a friend or how many papers to be read, when a woman entered, whether young or pretty, old or ugly, the gentleman vacated his seat and gave it to her. It was done as a matter of course. It was the custom. Is it so now? To some extent, but not so general as in times past. Take the trouble to notice the many tired females standing in our public conveyances. In the street cars you often see them swaying backward and forward, catching vainly at the strap which is too high for them, looking warm and red, and often indignant; for even now some are Quixotic enough to expect this act of chivalric politeness which was once so generally acceded the sex as their due.

Some excuses have been made for this growing change of custom. One is that ladies take the seat given by a tired man, worn out with walking and work, without even a "Thank you!" Suppose this be so: "Two wrongs don't make one right." Because a woman, weak-backed generally and weak-brained sometimes, forgets a few words of civility, must a man neglect the respect due always through mothers and sisters to all women. In New York and Philadelphia, a gentleman seldom yields his seat to a lady, unless she is young and handsome, but it is a good old Maryland custom that we hope to see retained. A few days since we observed a bright young girl jump up from her seat and give it to a venerable and tottering woman, whilst men sat still, without sympathy for her age and infirmities.

The jewel of Baltimore's park system is Druid Hill Park. The Madison Avenue entrance, left, welcomes visitors to 675 acres of rolling wooded landscape with eight lakes, playing fields, a zoo, tennis courts, a botanical garden, and many other features designed to offer respite from city life.

On June 19, 1888, the League of American Wheelmen held a bicycle race at Druid Hill Park. Competitors posed for a portrait in front of the Mansion House.

FOLLOWING PAGES:
Druid Lake, one and a half miles in circumference, gave Baltimoreans a relaxing pastoral setting in which to enjoy their leisure time.

Amusement parks were scattered all over the city and did an enormous business during their heyday before World War I. Riverview Park in southeast Baltimore was a popular attraction for thirty years—complete with Ferris wheel and roller coasters. In 1929 the park was razed to make way for Western Electric's Point Breeze manufacturing plant.

Recreation takes many forms in a city as diverse as Baltimore. Neighborhood organizations like the Mount Washington Club, right, provided a meeting place for large groups.

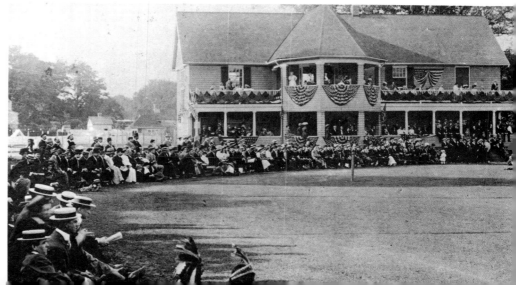

Playgrounds can be found in every neighborhood. The sliding board at Druid Hill Park apparently saw a lot of action.

In 1883 the American Association Brooklyn Athletics moved to Baltimore and became the Orioles baseball team. Oriole Park was the site of many games, including one between the Baltimore Gas and Electric Company team and its counterpart from Philadephia on July 17, 1909.

Junior players had to make due with more modest playing fields in city parks.

137

Two Years After

BY H. W. ATKINSON

from *The Book of the Royal Blue*, February 1906

On Sunday morning, February 7, 1904, at twelve minutes before eleven o-clock, the thermostat alarm connected with the six-story brick building occupied by J. E. Hurst & Co., as a wholesale dry goods and notion house, at German Street, Liberty Street and Hopkins Place, Baltimore Md., sounded an alarm of fire. The city fire-chief engineer reported as follows: "On entering the building the fire was discovered in the basement. As the men descended the stairs the daylight seemed to fade away, caused by the downpour of smoke through the elevator shaft, and immediately there was an explosion, the impact of which was upward and outward. The time between the receipt of the alarm and the explosion was about five minutes. The roof was lifted and every window light above the first floor was broken and flames shot out with a loud whistling noise. The concussion broke the windows in all the surrounding property and heavy brands of fire were carried from the Hurst Building to the adjoining property and at once seven buildings were burning fiercely. The wind at this time was blowing twelve miles an hour from the southwest and the streets here were thirty-five and forty feet wide. Brands of fire began to be blown several squares away setting fire to rubbish in yards and awnings, the flames of which immediately entered broken windows,

On February 7 and 8, 1904, the heart of Baltimore's business district was destroyed by fire. The conflagration began at the Hurst Building (the present site of the Civic Center), left. Firefighters came from Washington, D.C., Wilmington, and Philadelphia to help control the blaze, but the damage was widespread in spite of their efforts.

made so by the intense heat and the explosion of a box containing powder nearly opposite the Hurst Building."

It being Sunday and in a commercial district, there was no one to look after the numerous incipient fires. The fire followed the direction of the wind, which remained from the southwest until eleven o'clock at night when it changed to almost due west, and at noon on Monday changed to northwest. So great was the wind and the vacuum caused by the heat, that deluge streams were torn to fragments and could not reach the second stories. The conflagration raged until half past eleven Monday morning, February 8, in which time it had traveled over about 140 acres of ground and de-

More than fifteen hundred buildings were destroyed, but many were left partially standing. This made clean-up work particularly dangerous, and many of the precarious ruins were dynamited to remove them quickly.

stroyed eighty-six blocks, containing 1,526 buildings and four lumber yards, the estimated value of which was about $70,000,000, and the approximate insurance paid on the same being $29,221,851.51.

It was realized within thirty minutes after the first alarm that the fire was beyond the control of the Baltimore fire department and neighboring cities were called on for assistance, which was promptly and gladly given. There were engaged at the fire 460 firemen, twenty-four steam engines, eight hook and ladder trucks, one fire boat and one police boat, all belonging to Baltimore; there were also 771 firemen, thirty-three steam engines, two hose companies and one hook and ladder truck from other cities and towns. There were about 70,000,000 gallons of water used. During the twenty-four hours of the fire, although great risks were taken by the firemen, no lives were lost nor bones broken, but the Baltimore fire department lost one steam engine, one hook and ladder truck and about 30,000 feet of hose. In addition to sending over a large part of their fire apparatus, the city of Philadelphia also sent over a battalion of police to aid the Baltimore police department in preserving order, and they remained on duty until the local militia were called out and the city, within the territory of the burnt district, placed under martial law.

Before the fire was fairly out, plans were set on foot to turn what appeared to be a great calamity into what it is confidently hoped will be a lasting benefit to the city. An advisory committee was called together by the Mayor for a consultation as to what should be done. The result of their deliberations was the appointment of a Burnt District Commission to carry out a system of street and wharf improvements recommended by them. The committee was legalized by an act of the legislature, was appointed on March 11, 1904, and organized the following day.

The Baltimore & Ohio Railroad volunteered to lay temporary tracks to help clear out the debris from the great fire. Thousands of carloads of toppled brick and mortar were transported from the scene via Gay Street, above. New construction was already underway when the photograph below of Marsh Market Place was made just two months after the fire.

As soon as insurance matters could be adjusted the first necessity was the removal of the debris. The Baltimore & Ohio Railroad Company, with its tracks through the burnt district, promptly came forward with an offer to remove this debris, and temporary tracks were laid down and thousands of carloads of bricks and mortar were hauled away.

Generous offers of assistance poured in from every direction which the city authorities gratefully acknowledged but declined. The fire being in the commercial district, the number of families losing their homes was not large, but in order to take care of any destitution that had resulted, the State of Maryland authorized any part of a fund of $250,000 for the relief of such necessities.

But two years have passed since the great conflagration, but the phenomenal strides taken in rebuilding the city within that short time have far exceeded the sanguine hopes of the most optimistic citizen and established a precedent for the world.

Here are the results that have been accomplished. Of the 1,526 buildings destroyed, 1,343 were on the tax books for $12,908,300, the remainder being small out-houses and sheds not directly taxed. Allowing for the space used in street widenings, street openings and for the docks and the larger size of the buildings being erected, it is estimated that the number of the buildings in the burnt district, when entirely completed, will be about 800. So far 615 permits have been issued, representing buildings upon which the Appeal Tax Court have placed a valuation of about $20,000,000. It is interesting to note that the first permit for a building in the burnt district was issued in March immediately following the fire.

The high character of the buildings being erected in the burnt district has brought about building activity in other parts of the city, and a number of handsome apartment houses and office buildings are being constructed outside of the burnt district. The building of the Maryland Institute Schools of Art and Design was destroyed in the fire. Through a gift a large tract of ground has been secured on Mt. Royal Avenue in the residential district, upon which is now being erected a

In September 1906 Baltimoreans paused from their reconstruction efforts to celebrate all that they had accomplished in the thirty months since the great fire. The festivities were called Old Home Week, and thousands of out-of-towners came from far and wide to get a glimpse of the new, improved city. A parade in front of City Hall drew an appreciative crowd.

handsome building for the use of the art schools.

Thus Baltimore has accomplished within the short space of two years what many thought at the time of the fire would take years to accomplish. While large sums have been authorized for public improvements, more than two-thirds of the amount will go into improvements that will be self-supporting, and the increased value of property, with its increase in the taxable basis, will more than take care of the remainder. There can be no doubt that public improvements of the character of those already provided for and contemplated for Baltimore, must in time repay any reasonable outlay.

Much of Maryland's commercial and industrial life is centered in Baltimore. In 1940 the city was home to almost half of the state's population—a considerable work force. The port provided a variety of jobs, from servicing steamboats like the Emma Giles, right, to unloading lumber, coal, oysters, and watermelons.

Iron and steel and related industries were by far the highest earning businesses in Maryland according to the U.S. Bureau of Census figures for 1937. Bethlehem Steel's shipbuilding facilities, below, have provided jobs for thousands of Marylanders since they were established in 1891.

Industries that required skilled workers also made use of child labor throughout the nineteenth century. It is likely that the young boys pictured in the shop of the Central Millwork Company, above, toiled every day, perhaps even operating some of the woodworking machinery.

Food-related industries employed a large number of women, usually at low wages. By 1940 state law limited working hours for women to a maximum of ten per day in all occupations.

In the latter part of the nineteenth and early twentieth centuries thousands of children were employed in industries throughout the state—but especially in Baltimore. They worked in canneries and cotton mills, as seamstresses and straw hatmakers.

Photographer Lewis Hine documented the plight of the extremely poor, especially the migrant workers, in Maryland in 1909–10. He kept careful records of his subjects, and often his captions are as telling as the images themselves. Of the subjects below he wrote: "Three families is the rule in these shacks, one room above and one below, but sometimes four families crowd in."

The workers at left were employed by the J. S. Farrand Packing Company. Hine noted that "those too small to work are held in laps or closed away in boxes."

Many of the migrant workers were immigrants with few marketable skills and a formidable language barrier. During picking seasons, wagons would line up to transport the human cargo to the fields surrounding the city. The scene below took place on Wolfe Street near Canton in May 1910.

Some of the tasks performed by children were dangerous, like operating the canning machinery at left. Loss of life and limb was not uncommon. In the autumn of 1906 new laws came into effect which helped eliminate much of the use of child labor, and a compulsory school law ensured that the opportunity to learn to read and write was made available to all.

Practical Aviation

Latham's Record Flight Over Baltimore

from *The Book of the Royal Blue*, December 1910

The aviation meet at Baltimore during the first two weeks in November will probably be recorded as marking an epoch in practical aviation. With unprecedented obstacles in the way in the matter of foul weather and broken aeroplanes, the indomitable pluck of the aviators and courage of the managers under almost impossible adverse conditions was most commendable. Repairing their broken aeroplanes and flying in the face of fierce winds, which blew almost continually during the meet, the aviators established the fact beyond peradventure that aviation is practical and has come to stay.

The greatest achievement of the Halethorpe meet was the flight of Hubert Latham over a prescribed course above the city of Baltimore for a purse of $5,000, offered by the ''Sun'' and ''Evening Sun,'' of Baltimore, to give all the people of that great city an opportunity to witness the most remarkable scientific triumph of the present age.

It might be said in passing that this is also a remarkable age for advertising, and that the newspaper had a selfish end to accomplish. It most certainly had. The management of this old family newspaper of Baltimore wisely perceived that if this daring aviator who had the world at his feet could be persuaded to accept a prize to fly over the city where all the people, rich and poor, high and low, could see and behold, without money and without price, that it would be doing a lasting good thing for itself and a greater thing for the people; and, furthermore, if the flight was a success, that the amount of the prize money was incomparably small under these circumstances.

The flight was a success.

The day, November 7th, was perfect as November days go. The wind was blow-

On November 7, 1910, Baltimore became the first American city to witness the flight of an airplane. The management of the Sunpapers paid French aviator Hubert Latham five thousand dollars to dazzle 600,000 people with his daring achievement. Business came to a standstill, schools were dismissed, and thousands ascended to the rooftops of tall buildings.

ing and the air was crisp, but the sky was clear. At noon the great bell of the city hall clock chimed the prearranged warning that Latham had left Halethorpe and was on his way. Nearly six hundred thousand souls were anxiously watching and waiting. Business had stopped; schools were dismissed. Away out in the harbor whistles were shrieking, for up in the sky some 1,800 feet was a new thing—a great dragonfly—golden in the sunlight of mid-

day. Baltimore was seeing a new thing in transportation. Baltimore had invented the first practical railroad—the Baltimore & Ohio—the first telegraph and the first electric railroad. It was now gazing upon a new form of transportation that had been considered impossible for ages. Surely these were the latter days. It was uncanny; but wasn't it beautiful!

Steadily and gracefully Latham turned his street corners away up in the air. The people on the housetops and in the streets took off their hats and cheered. The sick in the hospitals were taken to the windows. At Johns Hopkins Hospital the great aviator dipped low to accommodate the patients because he said he would. On he winged his way like a great bird, following the course without deviation, and the people applauded.

It was from the top of the Baltimore & Ohio Building that the wonderful flight could best be seen, for the entire course of Latham's journey was in full view from the moment he arose above the mist in the Halethorpe region until he made his homing glide into it again.

Twice when he circled above it and the ''Sun'' Building faint cheers rippled up from the street, 225 feet below, and the cheer was taken up by the 600 spectators on the lofty roof; but the cheers died suddenly, for the awe that was inspired by this brave man's ride aloft there in the thin fluid of the atmosphere brought a lump into the throat and teardrops into the voice. So he sailed along on his creature of canvas and steel and got but the faintest inkling of the mild alarum that was sent up to his credit and glory.

Down on the streets far below, where the people looked like tiny insects, and to the clustering thousands upon the roofs radiating in every direction from this

Aviator Latham passed several of the city's landmarks during his historic flight.

Other pioneers of flight participated in the air show at Halethorpe. Here aviator Radley demonstrates his monoplane.

Latham's flight was part of an aviation meet held at Halethorpe in November 1910. A freak blizzard disrupted the show for four days. Many aircraft were severely damaged, but participants were determined to prove that the practicality of flight was not dependent on the elements; the planes were quickly repaired and the show went on.

massive Baltimore & Ohio Building, to the hundreds of thousands on the avenues, in the windows, in parks and gardens, in hospital wards and sickrooms, there never before was such a show. So simple was it, so free and popular, so general and so generous that it may be easily concluded that Hubert Latham had the greatest number of admiring spectators for his exhibition that ever any one man has had up to this time.

Yet the newspaper did not afterward shriek out its claim that "I did it." It paid

Latham's fellow pilots greeted him when he returned to the field at Halethorpe.

the $5,000 over to Mr. Latham and earnestly thanked him for his noble achievement on behalf of the people of Baltimore; and Mr. Latham modestly said he felt ashamed to take the money, because he had so much joy in the flight, fully realizing the emotions of the people below him. His faithful machine performed its duties without a hitch and he was safe.

Aviators are killed nearly every week in some foolhardy trick. There were prayers sent up for Latham's safety, because his performance was not a trick; it was a scientific triumph, and the thinking multitude realized the future would probably have even stranger things to show them.

Maryland's premier position in the history of aviation was assured in 1929 when the Glenn L. Martin Company relocated to Middle River on the outskirts of Baltimore. The site was selected for its proximity to Washington, its temperate climate that ensured year-round flying, the availability of skilled labor, and its access to the open water of the Chesapeake Bay for the testing of seaplanes. The first transoceanic commercial plane, the China Clipper, *was built by the Martin facility in March 1930. By 1940 the company employed twelve thousand persons and had achieved an international reputation for excellence. In recent years, through a merger, the concern became the Martin Marietta Corporation with offices in several locations in Maryland.*

The garment industry was a profitable one in Baltimore, due primarily to the sweatshops, which were later eliminated through the efforts of social reformers. More than a quarter of all manufacturing enterprises in the city were related to the clothing industry at the turn of the century, and 70 percent of the workers were Jewish.

In 1877 the first telephone arrived in Maryland at the electrical firm of Augustus G. Davis and Henry C. Watts. The two men were so impressed with their instrument that they began selling Bell's invention. The following year the Maryland Telephone Company of Baltimore City was chartered with Davis as its president. By 1893 there were three thousand subscribers in the state and the firm had become the Chesapeake and Potomac Telephone Company. At right, conduit construction for phone lines under 33d Street west of Abell Avenue was underway in 1914.

In 1816 Baltimorean Rembrandt Peale (son of the artist Charles Willson Peale) amazed onlookers with the first demonstration of the use of burning gas for illumination. Within a few months a business was formed to promote his invention: the Gas Light Company of Baltimore was the first gas company in the United States. Numerous competitive firms were established, but by 1906 it was determined that merging the various utility companies would make for greater efficiency, and Consolidated Electric Light and Power Company of Baltimore was formed. In 1955 the name was changed to Baltimore Gas and Electric Company.

The utility built its huge gas holding tank at Spring Garden in 1912. On July 13, left, the impressive size of the tank—222 feet high and 219 feet in diameter—was documented: on July 23, below, an interior view was made.

151

Transportation modes changed radically during the first quarter of the twentieth century. The transition from horsepower to gasoline engines was not instantaneous, however, as is dramatically demonstrated by the photograph of a horse-drawn gasoline ''truck,'' above.

Street hucksters come in many sizes and shapes in Baltimore. The display at right utilized an eye-catching technique to promote the benefits of apple consumption.

PRECEDING PAGES:
Baltimore made substantial contributions to the fighting effort in World War I. Its location close to the Atlantic—yet safely a hundred miles from the seacoast—made it ideal for shipbuilding and many new facilities were constructed to meet the demand. In 1919 Company I of the 115th Infantry participated in a victory parade in front of City Hall.

By 1922 the automobile was making its impression on the landscape in many ways. The Standard Oil station at the corner of Cedar and 33d streets was typical of gasoline station architecture for at least a decade.

Not only did the new vehicles require fuel, they also needed regular servicing. Automotive repair shops replaced the blacksmith shops of earlier times. Baltimore Gas and Electric Company maintained its own fleet of vehicles, and a sizeable maintenance facility, below, as well.

155

The oyster-packing industry was a large and prosperous one in Baltimore for many years. It gave employment to thousands dredging and shucking oysters, manufacturing cans and wooden crates, and building and repairing sailing craft. Skipjacks were a common sight at the Pratt Street oyster wharf in 1905, above.

Baltimore was home to two of the oldest silversmith firms in the United States. Samuel Kirk opened his shop in 1815 and quickly earned a reputation for exquisite craftsmanship. The Stieff Silver Company, right, also enjoyed a considerable following. In recent years the two establishments joined forces to become Kirk Stieff Company.

156

By 1931 many homes and most businesses had telephone service. The Depression forced many subscribers to give up the convenience, but the Chesapeake and Potomac Telephone Company responded by hiring teams of solicitors to call existing customers to convince them of the benefits of maintaining service. An average of 3,623 calls were made daily by each team.

Baltimore enjoys a long record of many firsts, including the first manufacturing of umbrellas in the United States. Polan, Katz and Company continued that tradition c. 1925. The tipping department, below, employed 220 women.

In August 1926 William Armstrong kept his customers at the Central News Stand abreast of world events—and well supplied with popular magazines and post cards, too.

Baltimore was on the move in the 1920s. Chesapeake Aircraft Company was just one of several aviation-related industries. The city had a number of runways, including a municipal airport on the harbor and the Martin Company's facility at Middle River.

Buses gradually replaced streetcars within the city, and for group travel outside the city limits buses became very popular.

BALT. TO GETTYSBURG

PRECEDING PAGES:
Baltimore developed impressively in the 1920s. An annexation in 1918 increased its area from thirty square miles to ninety-two square miles. What had once been green pastures became instead suburban communities. This aerial view taken c. 1925 shows the urban sprawl reaching ever outward.

Fort McHenry is almost as old as the nation itself. Named for Colonel James McHenry of Baltimore who was secretary of war from 1796 to 1800, the fortress saw its greatest moments in the War of 1812 when the city was attacked by the British fleet after it had burned much of Washington, D.C. While being held prisoner on an enemy sloop, Francis Scott Key was inspired to compose the poem "The Star Spangled Banner."

During the Civil War Fort McHenry was used to hold six thousand prisoners suspected of Southern sympathies, including the mayor of Baltimore and Francis Scott Key's grandson. From 1915 the fort was leased to the city for a park, but in 1925 the area was taken over by the National Park Service.

Fort McHenry is located on Whetstone Point overlooking the Northwest and Middle branches of the Patapsco River. In 1916 the Smith Flying Boat landed there and was stored at a nearby wharf.

162

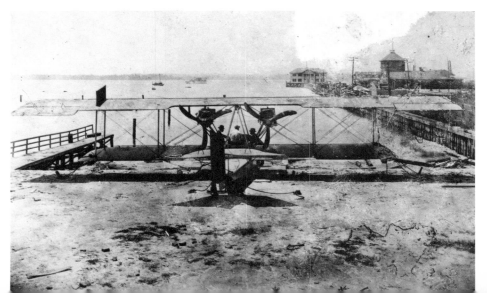

The harbor continued to be a busy place in 1935 when this aerial view was made, though the nature of the port had altered from its early days.

From the second half of the nineteenth century until well into the twentieth steamships were a primary form of transportation and Baltimore was an internationally known port. Numerous steamship companies lined Light Street, and their vessels served Boston, New York, Philadelphia, Savannah, Charleston, Wilmington, and New Orleans, as well as Havana and Liverpool. By 1910, when the photograph below was made, most of the remaining steamers traveled to destinations on the Chesapeake Bay and its tributaries.

SOUTHERN
Maryland

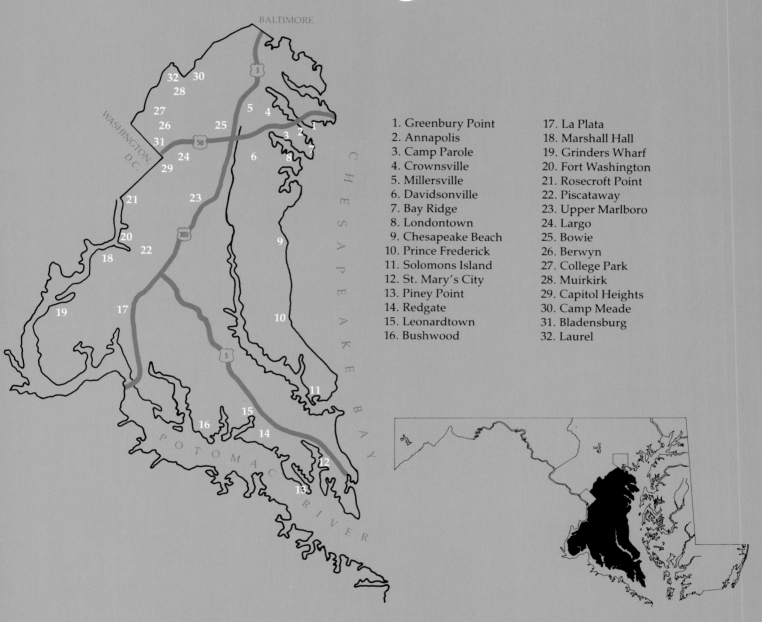

BALTIMORE

WASHINGTON D.C.

CHESAPEAKE BAY

POTOMAC RIVER

32 30
28
27
26 25
31
24
29
21
20
22
18
19 17
5 4
3 2 1
7
6 8
9
10
23
11
15
16 14
12
13

1. Greenbury Point
2. Annapolis
3. Camp Parole
4. Crownsville
5. Millersville
6. Davidsonville
7. Bay Ridge
8. Londontown
9. Chesapeake Beach
10. Prince Frederick
11. Solomons Island
12. St. Mary's City
13. Piney Point
14. Redgate
15. Leonardtown
16. Bushwood

17. La Plata
18. Marshall Hall
19. Grinders Wharf
20. Fort Washington
21. Rosecroft Point
22. Piscataway
23. Upper Marlboro
24. Largo
25. Bowie
26. Berwyn
27. College Park
28. Muirkirk
29. Capitol Heights
30. Camp Meade
31. Bladensburg
32. Laurel

Southern Maryland is surrounded and severed by water at almost every turn. Pleasure and work boats abound. Many inhabitants make their living from the bays, rivers, and creeks—fishing, dredging, studying marine life and naval sciences, building and repairing boats. This group of friends appears to have enjoyed an outing on Spa Creek in Annapolis in August 1916.

From Baltimore to Washington by Steamboat

BY OLIVER MARTIN

from *Chesapeake and Potomac Country*, 1928

A glimpse at the river;
And just a passing view
Of hamlets that were old
When our cities were new.

The distance from Baltimore to Washington, if you follow the route of a crow in flight, is about 40 miles, and you can cover that distance in an express train in something like 50 minutes. Or you can make the journey by steamboat, taking a day and two nights to make the trip and wandering through a large section of colonial America in doing it.

You leave Baltimore on Monday afternoon, for instance, and spend part of what is left of the daylight hours on the Patapsco River, which is another name for Baltimore Harbor, and Monday night on the broad waters of the Chesapeake Bay; during Tuesday and Tuesday night you are stopping at and starting away from various landings on the Potomac River, both in Maryland and Virginia, and you wake up on Wednesday morning at or near the wharf in Washington— 40 miles from where you started.

I made such a journey in the late summer of 1926, starting from Baltimore, although the start may be made from Washington if one prefers.

As the boat travels along the passengers begin making guesses as to her chances of winning a race that started when she left her pier, at which time three other steamers got the same notion. If you have ever been in Baltimore's inner harbor, you will recall the congestion there, with fussy little steamers coming in

Steamboat landings—both private and public—lined the Chesapeake Bay and its tributaries for more than a century. Not only did the sidewheelers provide transportation for human passengers; they also conveyed cattle, sheep, and other livestock, and tons of fresh produce from the Eastern Shore and Southern Maryland farms to markets in Baltimore and Washington, D.C.

In 1913 the steamer City of Baltimore *was fully outfitted with telephone service as it plied its way to Norfolk, Virginia.*

from and starting out for various points on the Chesapeake and its rivers and creeks.

The *Talbot* has made good headway and the others string along behind. The *Eastern Shore* is second, but the *Northumberland* passes her. Puffing along in the rear is the *Potomac*. But she gains foot by foot and eventually is abreast of us, within speaking distance. For a few minutes it is a bow-and-bow race, the Negro crews calling taunts to each other across the intervening stretch of water.

Slowly the *Potomac* pulls ahead and from her crew come bursts of triumphant laughter and yells of delight, mixed with expressions of amused contempt. Finally, one of the dusky fellows produces a rope

and shakes it in the direction of our crew. This is the crowning reproach. For every sailor knows that to "shake a rope at 'em" is the last word in insult—meaning, of course, that a ship at which a rope is shaken is in sore need of being taken in tow.

Fourteen miles from the city the river loses itself in the bay. And about here the passengers who have been on deck eagerly observing tramp steamers, schooners, bugeyes and other harbor craft realize that evening has stolen on them unawares, and that darkness is fast blotting out the distant shores.

But inside the boat there is plenty of light and activity, and downstairs in the dining room a hot chicken supper awaits appetites sharpened by salt sea breezes.

And as you sit there and talk with your friends, you dig up from memory's chests scraps of information about the great bay or perhaps your friends tell you about it.

The average person who has not sailed on this bay for a day or a night does not realize its size. It is 195 miles in length. The width at the upper part of the bay is from three to eight miles and in the lower part from 10 to 22 miles. Its greatest depth is 168 feet.

Flowing into the bay are 48 streams, most of them of a tidal nature, and ranging in length from two miles to more than 100 miles. These streams have in turn 102 branches, ranging in length from two to fifty miles. The streams and branches are all navigable and used for commerce, as the most shallow of them has a depth of about six feet, while the greatest depth, 156 feet, is found in the Patuxent River.

The combined length of the navigable waters comprising the bay, its tributaries and branches, is more than 1,750 miles.

The crew of the Chesapeake *posed for photographer Robert Sadler in July 1909.*

On account of the hundreds of indentations, as you can see by the map, Maryland has a very irregular shore line, and a long one. Swepson Earle figures the length of the Maryland shore line as 3,000 miles, and this excludes the creeks which are not navigable except at high tide.

Mr. Earle points out that if the shore line of the Chesapeake Bay country were stretched out in a straight line it would reach from the Atlantic to the Pacific and more than half the distance back.

Naturally, the area of the bay runs into big figures—more than 5,000 square miles.

A picturesque feature of the Chesapeake is the sailing craft, ranging from a long canoe to a five-masted schooner. There is one type of craft, the skipjack, that may be seen in fleets, scraping for crabs in Tangier and Pocomoke sounds and dredging in the bay and the Potomac for oysters.

In Chesapeake Bay language, the word ''canoe'' may mean, and frequently does, a sailing vessel with one or two masts, of a type that was in general use during the early days of the white men on the Chesapeake, when boats were made of hollowed logs. It is still in use, but in most cases the sails have been superseded or supplemented by a gasoline engine. In certain parts of the bay, where they are used in fishing, one may sometimes see a fleet of several hundred of them.

Another type of bay boat is the bugeye, the length of which ranges from 30 to 80 feet and of which both ends are sharp,

The Baltimore, Chesapeake and Atlantic Railway Company published the map at left in 1906. It is an extraordinary record of many communities once served by the steamship lines, some of which no longer exist. Note how far up the narrow rivers the boats traveled: steamship landings are indicated by black dots.

except in some cases where larger deck space is desired. The masts are set at a slant—that is, they rake to the stern—and it often looks to the observer as if the masts would snap off when under full sail. The bugeye is considered the swiftest sailing craft on the bay.

Some time during the evening our good ship passes over somebody's conversation, for the Chesapeake Bay is crossed by two submarine telephone cables, by means of which the people on the Eastern Shore are able to communicate readily and regularly with those across the bay. The first cable was laid in 1910 from Sandy Point on the Western Shore to Love Point on the Eastern Shore and crossed the narrowest part of the bay, about five miles. In 1916, an additional cable was laid across the bay, to take care of the increase in traffic.

Before the submarine cables were laid, long distance calls originating on the Eastern Shore of Maryland and Virginia for points on the Western Shore—Annapolis, Maryland, for instance, or Norfolk, Virginia—had to be routed all the way around the head of the bay, which sometimes necessitated a haul of three to four hundred miles in order to connect points which might actually be only fifteen to thirty miles apart.

But one must go to sleep sometime. At least, one sleeps until the first landing is reached, which is at Solomon's Island, at the mouth of the Patuxent. Then across the Patuxent to Millstone, where is unloaded a calf that protests in a loud and mournful voice.

While passengers are lost in slumber the boat makes a big sweep around Point Lookout, the extreme southern end of Maryland, leaving the bay and entering the wide mouth of the river.

Along about dawn, a few early birds among the passengers look out of their stateroom windows to watch the stevedores trundle off the merchandise for Wynne, formerly Miller's, on Smith's Creek, called Trinity Creek by Calvert in 1634 but later renamed by others in honor of Captain John Smith. Wynne is only a little settlement centering around a fish packing house and a cannery, but it stands on historic ground. Just back of the village is Calvert's Rest, marked by a fine old colonial dwelling, Calvert Hall, where lived William Calvert, son of the first governor.

Unless ice blocked the way, steamers met a year-round schedule. Below, a large crowd boarded the Maggie *on December 13, 1905.*

Awaiting the arrival of the steamboat gave neighbors an opportunity to visit and exchange news.

From Wynne the boat proceeds to St. Mary's City, or rather to the wharf, known as Brome's, near the site of Maryland's ancient capital, where Leonard Calvert and his little group of English Catholics established their town and proclaimed religious liberty throughout the colony. But St. Mary's City is no more. A church, a monument, a school, a wharf, a little group of houses and a beautiful view of the river—these are the things that may now be seen. In 1694, the Capital was removed to Annapolis, and from that year St. Mary's began to lose its prestige. Eventually, even the town itself disappeared.

As the boat slides up the next wharf, we read "Porto Bello" on the weather-beaten wharf house. Porto Bello recalls to mind the adventure of three Potomac River lads who sailed with Admiral Vernon of the British Navy as midshipmen in his campaign against the Spaniards in the West Indies, where they took part in naval engagements at Porto Bello and Carthagena.

When the young men returned to the Potomac and built themselves homes they incorporated into the names a reminder of their experiences. Lawrence Washington named his estate Mount Vernon, William Hebb called his place Carthagena and Edwin Coad borrowed the name of Porto Bello. All of these homes are still standing. The most famous, of course, is Mount Vernon, on account of George Washington, who inherited the place from his brother Lawrence.

The sun is now well up, shedding its brightness on the waters and lighting up the spire of St. Inigoes Church, seen through the trees in the distance. St. Inigoes; what an odd name! But when one considers that proper names were much corrupted 300 years ago in the everyday speech of the people, it is not surprising to learn that St. Inigoes was originally St. Ignatius.

Out of St. Mary's River we now take our way and steer directly across the Potomac to the Virginia shore, and enter the mouth of the Coan River, where are more wharves to be served and more history to be recalled.

Back to the Maryland side goes our good ship Northumberland, to do some more wandering among bays, islands and little rivers. It is now the middle of

A trip aboard a steamboat was not a speedy one. A few express boats did exist, but most stopped at every wharf of adequate size along the route.

the afternoon. We have been in the Potomac since dawn. Yet, on account of our meanderings on both sides of the river, we are still near enough to the mouth to see plainly the trees on Point Lookout, where the Potomac and the Chesapeake join.

At the mouth of the St. Mary's, where we were early in the morning, is St. George's Island, once noted as a summer resort. On crossing the Potomac in the afternoon, for a second visit to landings on the Maryland side, we pass to the north of the island, and touch at Piney Point, where there are several summer cottages.

If the voyager is seeking sheer beauty, he finds it here. The island is so close to the mainland that the shore seems continuous, as it curves around into a semi-circle of white, glistening sand, above which rise clumps of pine trees. Standing on the top deck of the boat and looking down on this scene, with a hot sun shining overhead, it does not take much imagination to conjure up thoughts of the South Seas.

Two hours of conversation and watching the scenery, and the captain remarks that we are approaching Leonardtown. But where? For no sign of a town can be seen. And then we learn that Leonardtown is not on the Potomac, but is hidden away at the edge of the hills that come down to the waters of Breton Bay, and that the steamer must do a lot of winding in narrow channels before the town is reached. And because groups of trees grow on every little neck of land, the wharf does not come in sight until the boat is almost upon it. Getting into Leonardtown is an adventure all by itself.

Next to St. Mary's, Leonardtown is probably the most historic place in Southern Maryland, and is probably more interesting to the present-day tourist than St. Mary's, for it has continued as a growing town ever since it was laid out in 1708. Furthermore, Leonardtown inherited much of the prestige that belonged to St. Mary's, for in 1710 the county seat was removed to the newer town, which was named for Benedict Leonard Calvert, fourth Lord Baltimore.

Leonardtown today is a quaint mixture of old and new. One may see colonial houses with massive brick chimneys and also little bungalows, and on the same street may be enjoyed the experience of passing ox-carts and Ford automobiles.

At the entrance to St. Clement's Bay, and seeming to prevent access to it, is Blackistone Island, originally called St. Clement's Island. Here Calvert and his little band first landed on March 25, 1634.

As the boat is leaving the bay the shades of evening are fast falling and the passengers gather in little groups on the top deck and watch the turning of the ship as she follows the channel, and listen to the captain as he explains the meaning of distant lights on the river or shore.

More sailing through the night, and the mouth of the Wicomico is reached, passing St. Catherine's Island and St. Margaret's Island. The influence of the Catholic colonists on the geographical names in Southern Maryland may be seen in the fact that even today a list of the towns, rivers, islands and bays sounds like a Litany of the Saints.

By the time the boat enters the Wicomico the evening is growing late, but there are still a few of the more inquisitive ones on deck as the landings at Bushwood and

Rock Point are reached, and the obliging captain turns his searchlight on the latter settlement, picking out of the night the little rustic church and other points of interest.

The Wicomico is one of the larger streams of Maryland and on it was once located the chief town of the Wicomico tribe of Indians.

During the rest of the night the ship plows its way steadily up the river, passing the point where Booth escaped into Virginia after shooting President Lincoln. The place where he crossed the river is near the mouth of Port Tobacco Creek, on which is located the ancient town of Port Tobacco, now only a group of picturesque old houses, hidden away in the valley. The town did not receive its name from the fact that much tobacco was shipped from there, as indeed it was, but from a young Indian queen, one of the earliest converts of Father White, a priest who

arrived with the first colonists. The name of the queen sounded like the word "tobacco" and tobacco it became.

It is interesting to note that Calvert in Maryland, like Penn in Pennsylvania, made friends with the Indians, and paid them for their lands. Not only did this kindly policy insure peace, but it speedily won the savages to Christianity. It is reported that Father White baptized the members of a whole tribe near Port Tobacco in 1642.

Also passed during the night is the big bend in the river at which the British fleet anchored during the War of 1812 while the troops it transported were laying in waste the newly built Federal City which we now know as Washington.

Another noted spot on the river in this neighborhood is Widewater, where Professor Langley, in 1896, gave his first demonstration of a heavier-than-air flying machine.

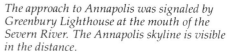

The approach to Annapolis was signaled by Greenbury Lighthouse at the mouth of the Severn River. The Annapolis skyline is visible in the distance.

Just above this place is the little town of Quantico, near which is one of the posts of the United States Marine Corps, and farther up, the Indian Head Proving Grounds.

Between Mount Vernon and Washington are two forts—one ancient and one modern. The ancient one, Fort Washington, is on the Maryland shore and was built in 1808 and destroyed by the British in 1814. It was rebuilt later but the equipment is now obsolete and it is probable that it will soon pass out of existence. The other, Fort Hunt, is on the Virginia shore and is equipped according to modern ideas.

By the time Alexandria is reached most of the passengers are up and dressed and out on deck, watching the river activities. Only a little farther now and the end of the journey will be reached.

Soon the boat enters Washington harbor and slides up to the dock. The passengers file ashore, having had the remarkable and delightful experience of making a journey of 40 miles in 40 hours in an age in which speed has been set up as something to which one should bow down and worship.

Tobacco was transported on steamboats in wooden barrels called hogsheads. Note that quite a few were lined up on the dock.

The oldest part of the Ancient City is centered around a narrow harbor known as City Dock. Main Street, right, leads to Church Circle, the site of St. Anne's Episcopal Church. Annapolis was planned primarily by Sir Francis Nicholson, the royal governor at the time the capital was moved from St. Mary's City. It was Nicholson's idea to lay out the city centered on two circles on the high knoll where the church and the State House would be built. It is the dome of the State House that dominates the skyline.

Steamboats arrived in Annapolis at the foot of Prince George Street, above. Capital of the State of Maryland since 1694, Annapolis is also the seat of Anne Arundel County. City and county were named for two different Annes: Anne Arundel was the wife of the second Lord Baltimore; Princess Anne, for whom Annapolis was named in 1695, later became Queen of England.

Middleton's Tavern, at the corner of Randall Street and Market Space, was built in the 1790s as a store and the Federal Customs House, right.

City Dock has always been a working harbor, lined with skipjacks and tonging boats in oyster season, and fishing and pleasure craft in the summer. Above, fishermen laid out their nets on the ground, perhaps to repair them. Middleton's Tavern and the Market House can be seen in the background.

The first Market House was built in Annapolis in 1728. In 1858 another market was built nearby, at the head of City Dock. It remains the hub of the city's commercial life. Market days c. 1885, left, attracted both buyers and sellers; local farmers delivered their produce in covered wagons.

Photographers quickly recognized the extraordinary vantage point provided by the dome of the State House for recording panoramic views. The c. 1870 view at right looks out to Spa Creek and the Chesapeake Bay beyond.

In 1890 Main Street in Annapolis was a pleasant mix of shops and residences. Business hours accommodated shoppers from 7:00 A.M. until 9:00 P.M. daily except Wednesdays, when many closed for the afternoon, and Saturdays, when most stores stayed open until midnight.

The Maryland State House, the third such structure on the site, was begun in 1772 but not completed until 1779. The elegant wooden dome, the largest in the country, was finished in 1788. The oldest state house in continuous use in the United States, the building was the setting for George Washington's resignation as commander-in-chief of the Continental army in 1783 and for the signing of the Treaty of Paris, which formally ended the Revolutionary War in 1784. The view at left was made about the turn of the century.

St. Mary's Hall, later a grammar school, on Duke of Gloucester Street is located on land that once belonged to Charles Carroll of Carrollton, signer of the Declaration of Independence and one of the wealthiest men of the Revolutionary period. His heirs willed the property to the Redemptorist order of priests, and a Catholic church and schools were built.

Governor Edwin Warfield and William Jennings Bryan, statesman and three-time-presidential candidate, were seated on the front porch of the Governor's Mansion when their portrait was made c. 1905.

Eastport, located across Spa Creek from Annapolis proper, was not annexed into the city until well after 1940. Situated between two wide creeks, the peninsula maintains its own identity even in modern times. In 1887 the citizens of Horn Point resolved to call their village "Severn City," but the name did not catch on. For many years the shoreline was dotted with boatyards like the one pictured above. Across the water part of the U.S. Naval Academy can be seen. The low dark vessel was the Santee, a training ship which sank at its dock in 1912.

The Annapolis harbor is often crowded with a motley assortment of boats. When photographer Henry Schaefer made the view at right c. 1890, even a canal barge was part of the transitory fleet.

176

FOLLOWING PAGES:
The route to Baltimore was improved considerably with the opening of the new drawbridge across the Severn River. An appreciative crowd assembled on a slope next to the Annapolis-side approach to the bridge to celebrate its dedication in the summer of 1924.

The charm of Annapolis attracted the attention of many gifted photographers. In 1893 Frances Benjamin Johnston was commissioned by the U.S. Navy to visually document life at the Naval Academy for a series of albums that were displayed at the Columbian Exposition in Chicago. One of the delightful scenes she recorded was the street huckster selling strawberries in the academy.

One of the more popular picnic spots in the Annapolis area was Horseshoe Curve where the community of Wardour later was developed. Families would pack up all sorts of paraphenalia and cart it to the wooded area protected by a bluff, complete with a sandy beach on the Severn River and a fresh water spring. Photographer Henry Schaefer, who had a studio on Main Street in Annapolis from 1888 until his death in 1895, enjoyed a tranquil afternoon at Horseshoe Curve.

Every summer Maryland's famous blue crabs wander up the Severn River from the Chesapeake Bay. Crabbers young and old keep a watchful eye—and a net handy.

177

The Meredith Lumber Company was doing a booming business at the foot of King George Street in 1923.

For more than half a century the Henry B. Meyers hardware store in the first block of West Street kept Annapolis well stocked with tools, supplies, and appliances.

Far right, in September 1927 Native Americans of the Blackfoot Nation from Glacier National Park arrived at the U.S. Naval Academy. They were on their way to Halethorpe in Baltimore County to participate in the Fair of the Iron Horse, the centennial celebration of the Baltimore & Ohio Railroad.

The Annapolis Dairy was located on the site of the first train station in the city, that of the Annapolis & Elkridge Railroad. Later the location became the home of the local bus station.

In the 1930s the Middleton's Tavern building had been architecturally modified and converted into a confectionary. Over the years the structure has been home to many businesses other than the tavern: a meat market, a liquor store, a gift shop, and a restaurant have all occupied the building at the corner of Randall Street and Market Space.

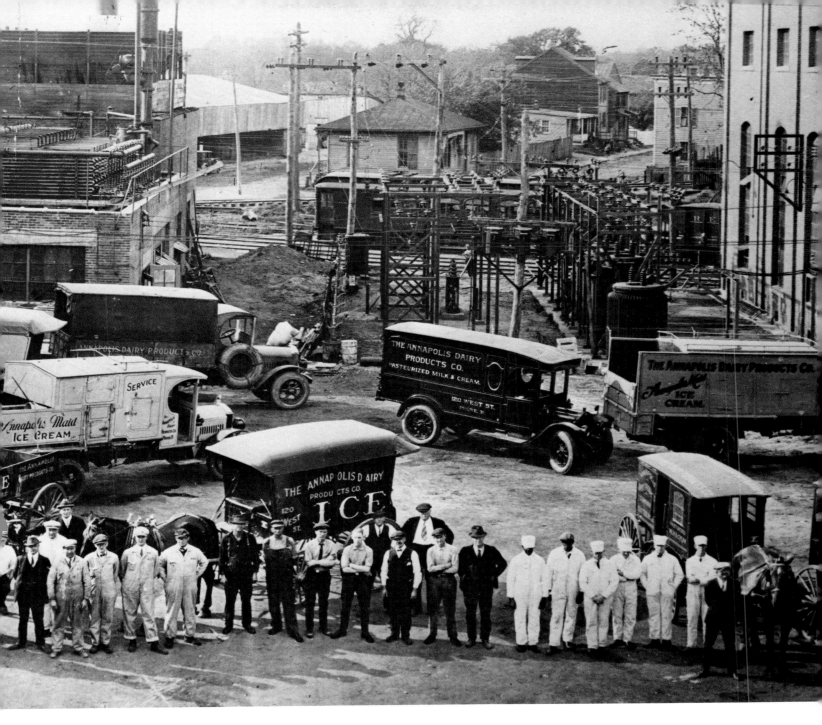

Eastport had become heavily populated by the 1930s. The shore—bordered by Spa Creek, the Severn River, and Back Creek—was lined with boats. Trumpy's Boatyard, which constructed some of the most famous yachts of the period, was located in the large, white-roofed structure near the center of the aerial photograph, left.

The Annapolis Yacht Club, located on Compromise Street at Spa Creek near the mouth of the Severn River, was originally housed in a small shack and was actually a rowing club called the Severn Boat Club. By the 1930s its quarters had enlarged considerably, right.

In the summer of 1931 a photographer from the Keystone View Company climbed the 149 steps of the State House dome to make the photograph below. The scene looks down Francis Street and illustrates the lower half of Main Street and the City Dock area. Spa Creek and Eastport are seen in the distance.

Annapolis began to develop its suburbs in the beginning of the twentieth century. The improvements underway on West Street at Lafayette Avenue c. 1910, above, were a sign of the times. Nearby Murray Hills was considered the outskirts of town in that era.

The only known photograph made at Camp Parole in the Civil War period survives as a carte de visite made by J. L. Winner between 1864 and 1866, left. The United States government established the facility in 1863 to hold Union prisoners paroled by the Confederates until they could be returned to active duty. Prior to the establishment of the camp, it was suspected that soldiers were allowing themselves to be captured so that they could return home on parole. About seventy thousand men passed through Camp Parole. The average daily population was close to eight thousand.

Annapolis

BY HILDEGARDE HAWTHORNE

from *Rambles in Old College Towns*, 1917

*A*nnapolis is as clean and bright as a new whistle, in spite of its dignified age, witnessed by the innumerable stately mansions that speak a day when men built houses that matched a courtlier time and more gracious manners than we know to-day, when they built for a family, for sons to succeed them, and set their homes within gardens whose large leisure reflected their own spirit, unhurried, never idle, serene. Within its small extent Annapolis has more of these fine old homes than any other place in America. It has also been a sailor town so long it must be as spic and span as it is old and noble—there is the air of a quarterdeck to Annapolis.

The little city is almost surrounded by water and the breath of the sea is sweet across it. Its greatest interest, next to its own existence, is the fact of the Naval Academy, of whose fine portals, with the dome of its Chapel, you constantly catch glimpses, now down some tree-embowered street, now across a little square, or beyond blue water and clustering fishing craft from an old wharf—and the old wharves are a mighty pleasant section of a most adorable town.

The centre of all is the State House, a square Colonial building with a white cupola and noble portico, that stands on a slight rise, the avenues and streets leading to it from the radius of a circle, and a flourishing little park surrounding it.

The Liberty Tree on the front campus of St. John's College derives its name from the meetings of the Sons of Liberty held under its branches before the Revolution. The tulip poplar is thirty feet in circumference and is thought to be at least four hundred years old. Its trunk has been hollow since before 1840 when local boys set off gunpowder in the opening and set the tree ablaze. The fire was extinguished and the prank turned out to be a blessing: the following year its foliage was better than ever—parasites had been destroyed in the heat. In 1907 the mayor of Annapolis, Gordon Claude, assembled his children and their friends in the hollow of the tree for this amusing portrait.

Close by are the Governor's House, old churches, the court house, in fact, the whole group of public buildings, and many of the finest mansions. But truly everything is close to it, for the town is as compact as it is small; a morning's stroll will take you all over it, from the line of the old Civil War fortifications and the site of the one-time gate to the Severn River and Annapolis Harbor, from College Creek to Spa Creek.

The Naval Academy is by no means the whole of Annapolis. There is St. John's College, lying just across from the upper part of the reservation, the two being separated by King George Street. This college was founded as King William's School in 1696, the first free school in America. Its main building, McDowell Hall, was begun in 1742, and then intended for the governor's residence, but for some reason the intention remained unfulfilled.

St. John's College, successor to King William's School, which was established in 1696, is one of the oldest institutions of higher learning in the United States. During the Civil War the campus was transformed into a military hospital, but classes resumed with the peace. On February 20, 1909, when the school was about to celebrate its 125th anniversary, a disastrous fire (probably caused by defective wiring) destroyed the most historic structure on the campus, McDowell Hall. The entire brigade of midshipmen from the Naval Academy came to help, but with little success. The building exceeded the reach of local firefighting equipment, so the hoses were hoisted up into the surrounding trees. Although many wanted to raze the ruins and construct a modern replacement, the colonial building was restored the following year.

St. John's was the Alma Mater of Francis Scott Key, as a bronze tablet in the façade of McDowell Hall relates. And there is another special possession of the college, the great Liberty Tree, standing on the campus part way up the slope. This tree is a tulip, and of enormous size. It is a forest in itself, and as we stood under it, looking up into the vast spread of branches, and listening to a world of birds singing among the innumerable leaves, it appeared rather like the tree of some ancient folk tale than an actual plant. Its age is unknown, but under its boughs a treaty between the Susquehannock Indians and the first white settlers of that locality was drawn up. Since that day it has seen countless political gatherings; here the early settlers made rendezvous to consider plans for defence, here Washington and Lafayette walked in earnest talk, and beneath it the French tents were pitched in Revolutionary days. Apparently it has always been a notable tree, older and larger than any other, in all that countryside.

Annapolis is full of old and beautiful relics of past days. Fire has wrought less destruction here than in most of our Colonial cities. Only a few years younger than ivy-hung St. John's, where for

English, and charmingly patterned. The spacings of walls and windows are managed in masterly style, and though the windows are not large, the whole effect carries elegance. A pointed pediment flanked by two chimneys surmounts the second story above the pillared portico, and above all soars the dome, a curious structure in its detail but most agreeable to the eye. From the top of this dome we looked out on the whole of the little city, ringed by its blue and silver waters and dressed in the green finery of hundreds of trees. There lay the Academy, a lovely pattern; there old St. John's, close beside us the ancient church of St. Anne, and amid fair gardens the fair houses of the brave men and noble who had made the capital their home through the long history the town has known.

It was in this building, in the old Senate Chamber, that Washington surrendered his commission as Commander in Chief, and that, a year later, the Treaty of Peace with Great Britain was signed and delivered. The room has been kept in the same condition, with the desk over which the

liam of Orange, and left Anne childless. And each street has its wonderful old houses, some set far back from the quiet street, some closely edging it and walling the view from the magnolia-planted garden behind. Inside, we were told, are doors and mantels carved by hand—the mantelpiece of the Brice mansion had an international reputation, and the house is notable even in that town of notable homes, with its great, flat end-chimneys, its high pitched roof, the wings connected by corridors and buried in ivy. Then the Chase House, the finest specimen of its type in all America, famous for the silver mounted mahogany doors, the great double staircase with its classic pillars and the chimney pieces carved with scenes from Shakespeare's plays. This wonderful house, whose carved breakfast room was fit for kings to eat in, is now used as an old people's home. It is pleasant to think of the old folk finishing their days in a house whose own age is like a benediction.

The Peggy Stewart House, close to the Naval Academy, is the spot made notable by the fact that there Peggy watched her husband [father], Anthony, set fire to his brig with his own hands as a peace offering to his enraged townsfolk. For he had come to port of an October day in 1764, laden with tea—and tea was not being drunk in the Colonies then.

Idling along we found ourselves at the end of Main Street, where an arm of the harbor came up to a little round park in the middle of which was a well curb, with the dates 1649–1708 cut into the stone. But though we asked several passersby, no one knew what they signified. Later we found that it was here that ten families of persecuted Puritans, crossing the Potomac to the Severn side, built huts, taking advantage of the Toleration Act, the glory of Maryland under Governor Stone. So part of the date was accounted for. It was in 1608 that that intrepid discoverer, Captain John Smith, first sailed up Chesapeake Bay—perhaps we had misread the second date.

Close to the park is the fish market, and if there is anything more worth seeing than a fish market, why, I remarked to Sister, bring it on. There, in shining rows and heaps lay the flashing catch of the sea. Heaped in baskets were oysters—Annapolis has a big trade in oysters, packing away barrel upon barrel of the famous Chesapeakes. Salty men hung about, wearing battered hats and blue shirts, and mumbled to each other, indifferent to the rest of the world, as is the fashion of elderly sailor- and fishing-folk. Beyond extended the wharves and docks, crowded with small boats and smacks. Dogs lay in the sun, and small brown children played about.

Over the years radical architectural changes have been made to several State-owned buildings. The photograph above shows the back side of the State House before the annex of 1902–10 was added. It also shows the original design of the Governor's Mansion, finished in 1870 and very much an example of that period's Victorian styles. In 1935 the structure was "Georgianized" to be more in keeping with the city's eighteenth-century mansions.

awhile we watched the collegians drilling on the campus, is the State House, that stands on the highest part of the peninsula on which Annapolis is built, within the green circle of its parked grounds. The present building was begun in 1772, and is one of the finest expressions of the architecture of its noble period. The bricks that went to its making are

resignation was tendered still in position. A great painting of the event is hung on the wall, and portraits of the four Signers of the Declaration of Independence who were citizens of Annapolis, Stone, Chase, Paca and Carroll of Carrollton.

"Walking through these streets and lingering by these old houses is very much like opening a volume of our early history and stepping into it bodily," remarked Sister, as we sauntered along the leafy ways. The very names of the streets belong to another day. King George and Prince George, Cornhill, Hanover, Calvert (family name of Lord Baltimore), Carroll. Here too is a Gloucester Street, that used to be Duke of Gloucester named after the same child honored in Williamsburg, whose early death struck the joy from the heart of his father, Wil-

Not far away was a place that had a sign out, *Sea Food*. To that spot we went in haste, and presently the oysters were proving their worth to us. Oh, the poor, tasteless creatures eaten in the white glare of Broadway! The pitiful apologies that lie, tame and spiritless, on beautiful china in the rich hostelries of Fifth Avenue. More terrible still, those flaccid canned abominations of the West.

Once again we resumed our lazy tour of the town. We didn't want to miss seeing Carvel Hall, the old Paca homestead, and now a hotel. It is a five minute walk from the fish market, on Prince George Street, and as soon as we saw it we wished that we were to spend a long while in Annapolis, and that Carvel Hall were to be our headquarters. Here the mothers and sisters of graduating students come, and from it go joyous girls to the dances at the Academy. William Paca

Annapolis boasts a rich concentration of several of America's most elegant colonial homes. The Brice, Chase-Lloyd, Hammond-Harwood, Ridout, Peggy Stewart, and Scott houses are all part of the legacy of the period when Annapolis was the social as well as political center of the state. The William Paca House, above, has the added attraction of its beautifully restored formal and wilderness gardens. This view of the rear of the mansion was made before 1890. In 1899 the house became the nucleus of the famed Carvel Hall Hotel.

was one of the governors of Maryland as well as a Signer of the Declaration, but splendid as might have been his other attainments, he never did anything finer than the building of this house, with its two wings, its air of gracious welcome and warm dignity, a house that has an unforgettable personality aside from its

sheer beauty. The very wall that guards it from the street is a work of art.

"And in all the little city," remarked Sister, "there is not one shabby spot, not a minute of disorder or decay. Fresh and clean it is as this shining water and sweet as the sea wind. It has all that's best in being old and nothing that is not best."

You could not walk a street that did not have something worth notice on it. On our way back to Church Circle to take the car we turned into little Charles Street to look at the quaint gable-end house and printing office where Jonas Green lived and published the Maryland Gazette, founded by him in 1745, the first in the colony. And as the car was not yet due we took the few steps that separate Church from State Circle to gaze upon the old Governor's Mansion, new for Annapolis, being built in 1867, but an attractive place standing in flower-planted grounds and finely shaded, like the rest of the city.

The sun was setting in purple and gold as we turned back to the car line. From the direction of the Naval Academy came a faint echo of music, then the boom of a gun. The day was over.

"We have seen the most perfect town Colonial America produced," said Sister.

One architectural gem, later lost, was the first governor's mansion, which was located on the grounds of the Naval Academy. For many years it was the residence of the superintendent. An intimate glimpse at the midshipmen's social life is provided by this photograph of a tea party held in the parlor of the original Government House c. 1893.

The United States Naval Academy was founded in Annapolis in 1845 on the site of Fort Severn, which had been an army post. The school has a proud heritage of training professional naval officers, uninterrupted except for the Civil War when the students and faculty were transported to Newport, Rhode Island, because Southern sympathies in Annapolis were considered a threat. For the duration of the war the grounds were transformed into a hospital. At far left, students get hands-on experience during a seamanship drill in 1893.

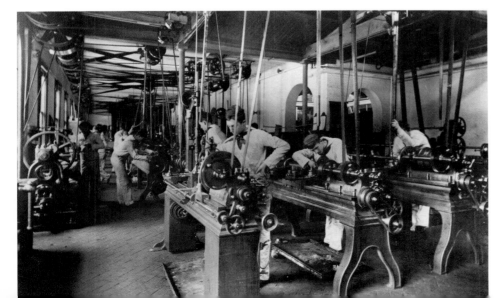

For many years engineering was the only major course of study open to students at the academy. Training was primarily geared toward technical subjects. When photographer Frances Benjamin Johnston was assigned the task of making an official record of the school in 1893, she portrayed the naval cadets (as they were called at the time) in mechanical drawing class, far above, in a sham battle, above, and at work in the machine shop, left.

Students were well prepared for all aspects of naval life. For many years steam engineering was an important part of the curriculum, and cadets learned both to build and repair engines. Navigation, surveying, and telegraphy were among other courses taught.

The young men relaxing at right in 1903 were among the first academy students designated as "midshipmen" in many years. In 1870 the title of "midshipman" had been changed to "cadet-midshipman," and two-year students (an option at the time) were called "cadet engineers." All students became "naval cadets" in 1882. In 1902 the term "midshipman" was reinstated.

The class of 1939 faced an uncertain future following their graduation, held in Thompson Stadium, below. Less than three years later their training would be put to the ultimate test as they served their country in World War II.

The social life of midshipmen was carefully regulated. Their busy schedules allowed for little free time. Occasionally a major event would alter the routine. When Prince Henry came to visit in 1902, all the ladies—probably officers' wives and daughters—donned their finest gowns, left. They awaited his arrival on the porch of the superintendent's residence.

The high point of every academic year was June Week, and one of the major events of those festivities was the color-girl parade, above. Hundreds of young women descended upon Annapolis each year to attend gala balls and tea parties. The modern tradition of wedding bells at the close of June Week was not part of the program before 1940. Midshipmen were forbidden to marry until they had served at least two years in the Navy after graduation.

The mood at graduation in 1902 appears to have been quite jolly. President Theodore Roosevelt, the featured speaker, joined in the joke, left, as the first classmen received their commissions as ensigns.

PREVIOUS PAGES:
Facilities for the mentally ill in Anne Arundel County were racially segregated. Crownsville State Hospital for Negroes was established in 1911. Both male and female patients received training in farming techniques, basket making, rug weaving, and other crafts.

The countryside south of Annapolis remains largely agricultural in nature. Around the turn of the century, leisure time appears to have been passed in simple yet pleasant ways.

The gathering of the clan at Bunker Hill in Millersville was quite an event in 1896, above.

The harvest was over, but it was apparently still warm enough for a picnic lunch.

196

The appropriate frock was required for an outing in the family automobile near Davidsonville in 1913.

This charming scene was probably made on the South River. It must have been lovely when the water lilies were in blossom.

Bay Ridge

BY EVANGELINE KAISER WHITE

from *The Years Between*, 1957

Our summer amusements were more numerous and much more enjoyable because work lessened and most families could plan their pleasures together. The greatest one was our fabulous Bay Ridge, name of charm and promise that still recalls the thrill of my childhood joy in anticipation of a real gala excursion and outing on the shores of our beautiful Chesapeake Bay. There was never anything like it, and I can say, without fear of contradiction, there has never been anything comparable to it up to now on our Chesapeake Bay. The place you see today still bearing the name Bay Ridge, developed into a summer residence area, is still a lovely situation on this high promontory with its long line on the Bay, and around the corner the lovely Severn River reaching right to Annapolis and the Naval Academy. But this is *not* the Bay Ridge of seventy years ago which I am going to describe to try to give you a bit of the thrill I experienced, which is gone forever. Even the very ground upon which this fabulous amusement park and resort was built was all washed away, gradually slipping into the Bay and being carried away. The place was developed by the B. & O. Railroad as a resort for the people of Washington and Baltimore, and the Railway's steam engines and coaches provided the only way by land for people to reach Bay Ridge. Baltimore ran excursion boats which landed at the end of a huge pier which stretched far out into the Bay. The boats were very large and carried hundreds of people. One was named *Louise*, one the *Columbia*, and the other the *Emma Giles*, and they always came crowded to their "gunnels" with people. This place was developed in the Gay Nineties when everything was done in a big and lavish way, especially if railroad magnates were doing it, so I hope you can catch some idea of its

Bay Ridge resort was established in 1882 by the Baltimore & Ohio Railroad as an excursion spot for the people of Baltimore and Washington. Although located only a few miles from Annapolis, for many years Bay Ridge could be reached only by train or steamboat. The resort was equipped with every modern convenience: a large hotel, an enormous pavilion, a restaurant that could accommodate several hundred people at a time, and a bandstand with acoustics so good that the music could be heard anywhere on the grounds.

beauty and magnitude and not feel my description is an exaggeration of childhood's memory. The railroad came into the resort back of all the park; this today is the road on the front of the Bay shore drive. Everything that was on the Bay side of that drive which now enters Bay Ridge is gone—washed away forever.

Across the whole front were a boardwalk and a pavilion reaching from one end to over half of the space of the other end of that vast expanse of Bay front. I have never seen anything like it. It was tier on tier of long, gradual steps rising to the first level about twelve feet high. Here were concessions of soft drinks and ice-cream stands, souvenir stands, the restaurant and picnic tables and chairs. The upper decks were reached by two smaller sets of stairs, one on either end. The top roof was bright red with cupolas and pinnacles with flags floating in the breeze from every flagstaff they held, and there was always plenty of breeze blowing to make them stand out all aflutter. Such a gala scene was presented to the hot passengers as the train approached the pavilion! Under this pavilion were housed Jolly's Waxworks,

freak exhibits, sculpture, and a huge photography studio. Right in front of these long, low pavilion steps was a bandstand, a most ornate shell affair. Here band concerts would be given, dancing schools from Baltimore used to stage dance recitals, and vaudeville actors would do their stunts. The audience would sit on these steps and see everything from there, as all was out of doors and free to anyone at the resort. At the right end of the pavilion were the bathhouses with a real toboggan or slide right down into the water from that high bluff; but of course there were railing steps to walk down to the lovely white sand beach below for the faint-hearted who could not brave the slide.

Following the boardwalk to the other side of the pavilion there was a wide-open space and at the end of that was a big ornate gay nineties hotel. Here were confined whatever gambling and drinking were done; in that way these activities were limited to a very small number of people–only those wealthy enough to

Bay Ridge enjoys a spectacular location on the Chesapeake Bay at the mouth of the Severn River. Every year thousands of vacationers arrived on steamboats and made their way up the wharf, which extended far into the Bay since the water near the shore was quite shallow. The sandy bottom and the shallow depths made for excellent swimming: in fact, there were 426 individual bath houses in which to change into one's bathing costume.

patronize the hotel. Thus the large groups of excursionists who came by boat or train with their families and children, and who patronized the resort, were not exposed to this part of it. That is what kept the tone of the place on such a gay and high level, making it a safe place for families to have their outings. Sad to say, there came the inevitable time of the raising of Prohibition, and deterioration began, as is always the case without fail. Of course God in nature finished it by erosion. The long pier which was reached by going down the embankment about fifty steps was built out about a thousand feet into the water, far enough to float the large excursion boats. The end of the pier was broadened and covered over for the fishermen and crabbers, as those sports were among the chief attractions for the water devotees. On the other side of the railroad track, right behind the pavilion and hotel, were the picnic grounds and amusement park. Here there were tables and benches among shade trees, and the flying horses, shooting galleries, Ferrris wheel, and gravity road. This gravity road ran way back to Lake Ogleton, where it would stop and let off passengers who wanted to take a boat ride on the Lake.

Can you wonder that a promise from our parents to take us on a picnic or day's outing to Bay Ridge, to this paradise, just thrilled us to our toes? Yes, we were willing to settle for that paradise, the intermediate place, rather than heaven. The excursion train for Bay Ridge would leave Bladen Street Station. We would be backed out of the station, cross the College Creek Bridge, all the way back to West Annapolis and sometimes nearly to Wardour, depending upon how many coaches were attached. Then, as the engine reached the Y, it would be swung open and we would be switched to the other track. The engine would then be in front and start ahead, pulling the coaches over the short bridge span right across West Street out what is now our Amos Garrett Boulevard, over another bridge at the head of Spa Creek, and then on down to Bay Ridge. How we loved the excitement of that ride, to go out of Annapolis at Bladen Street and to see ourselves shortly afterward back in Annapolis again, at the tip end of West Street, was always a joke to us.

The view from the pavilion at Bay Ridge was exceptional. Erosion has destroyed much of the high bluff on which the resort was built. Concessions of all sorts catered to the whims of visitors. A gravity railway, a Ferris wheel, steeplechase races, and a merry-go-round were just a few of the amusements available. Fishing and crabbing from the long pier were popular pastimes, and sailboats could be rented.

Bay Ridge declined as a resort with the advent of prohibition. The area was then developed into a summer residential community. Nearby Arundel on the Bay afforded a clear view back to Bay Ridge, obviously appreciated by the photographer, above. A steamboat can be seen at the end of the long pier. Note the train tracks of the Columbia Street Railway on the sand.

In 1900 the resort was converted into the Chesapeake Chautauqua. Regular lectures were offered by the Chautauqua Literary Scientific Circle, and diplomas were conferred on those who completed the course of study. There were also nondenominational camp meetings. The Book of the Royal Blue, published by the B & O Railroad, declared in 1900 that ''the intellectual and moral influence which will exist, removing as it does the objectionable features which seem an unavoidable accompaniment to so many excursion places, coupled with all the attractions of this famous resort make the Chesapeake Chautauqua unusually attractive and leave no doubt of a phenomenal success in the future.''

Anne Arundel County below Annapolis is the unofficial border of true Southern Maryland. Traditions are sacred in this region. The South River Club, right, for example, is reputed to be the oldest social club in the United States. Beginning in 1772 (or perhaps earlier), members have met several times a year—except between 1874 and 1895, when no meetings were held. In modern times the club has met four times yearly. Membership is limited to descendants of clubmen. Occasionally guests are invited to join in the all-day feasting, as must have been the case c. 1907 when this photograph was made. The gentleman standing behind the empty chair is Governor Edwin Warfield.

Tulip Hill, above c. 1900, is an excellent example of five-part Georgian architecture. Begun in 1756 by Samuel Galloway, a wealthy Quaker merchant, the house has several unusual features, notably the double-hipped roof and chimneys formed into arches, a rare style in the colonial period.

London Town Publik House, right, is all that remains of the once thriving community where the Anne Arundel County Court met from 1689 to 1695. At the time this photograph was made the building served as the county almshouse.

The farmers of Anne Arundel County are famous for their annual crop of plump, ripe strawberries, like those at far right grown in 1928.

Chesapeake Beach, as its name suggests, is located right on the Bay, just over the line into Calvert County. The steamer Dreamland began its service between Baltimore and Chesapeake Beach in 1912 and continued until 1925. The resort community had enjoyed a promising beginning in June of 1900 when its grand amusement park was formally opened. Less than a month later, however, a fatal accident on the Chesapeake Beach Railway dampened the enthusiasm of potential visitors and the park never achieved the popularity hoped for by its founders.

Official U.S. Post Office records show that a post office was established at Chesapeake Beach on June 12, 1894. That operation lasted only nine days. It reopened on March 21, 1899.

A published history of the local railway describes Chesapeake Beach as ''a modest cottage community with an amusement park.'' One can only hope that the scene at left was not the prelude to a domestic tragedy.

Most excursionists who arrived via steamer were from Baltimore. Washingtonians came on the struggling Chesapeake Beach Railway by way of Hyattsville. The long pier was necessary because the water was much too shallow nearer shore for the large steamboats.

By the 1920s, automobiles had made travel to the ocean resorts on the Eastern Shore a reasonable and exciting alternative for family outings. Chesapeake Beach continued its decline, but the owners refused to give up. In 1928 they decided to make substantial improvements and removed part of the boardwalk. Renamed Seaside Park, it opened its gates in 1930. Even if the new attractions had caught the public's interest, the state of the economy would have precluded any real success for what very soon became a frivolous and impossible expense for most families.

There was only one hotel at Chesapeake Beach, the Belvedere, above. On March 30, 1923, it and several other buildings burned to the ground. The decision was made not to rebuild since the resort had always had the most appeal for one-day visitors.

The original boardwalk was a mile long and lined with refreshment stands and concessions. The boardwalk was built on piers parallel to the bluff about three hundred feet from shore.

Cottages were available for rent during the summer season. Most had spectacular views of the Chesapeake Bay.

It was apparently a fine day for fishing when this photograph was made. The amusement park can be seen in the distance.

Swimming in the Bay was not always a pleasure. Stinging nettles, which arrive in the water each summer, can cause considerable discomfort. One of the improvements made in the late 1920s was the construction of a large salt-water bathing pool.

Games of chance were a favorite way to spend money. Besides the many concessions where prizes were awarded, a casino operated at Chesapeake Beach. One can only wonder how many parakeets survived the trip home on the steamboat or train.

Other prizes were even more extravagant—real silk stockings. A racecourse was part of the original plan for the resort and was actually constructed in 1900, but it never opened, probably because the necessary permits could not be obtained. It was dismantled and the materials were used elsewhere at the park.

No trip to a resort would be complete without a photographic record of the occasion. Doubtless many visitors stopped by the gallery to have their pictures made—printed right on a picture post card to send to the unfortunate friends who did not get to share the excursion.

Far right, for the strong-of-heart, the most popular attraction at the amusement park was the roller coaster built right out over the water. The alternative for those with more delicate constitutions was a charming carrousel built by Gustav A. Dentzel, complete with a Wurlitzer band organ.

208

Calvert County is a peninsula that was isolated for many years because it lacked a bridge across the Patuxent River to link it with its neighbors. It is Maryland's least populated county, originally settled by Puritans from Virginia. The seat of government, Prince Frederick, was attacked by the British in 1814, and totally destroyed by fire in 1882. At right, every year George Turner and several of his friends from Prince Frederick would rent a schooner and escape for a week of sailing on the Bay. Their cruise c. 1930 appears to have been a relaxing one.

Solomons Island is at the southern end of Calvert County. It has long been a popular sport fishing community. The harbor on the Patuxent River is two miles wide and 150 feet deep.

The Drum Point Lighthouse signaled the mouth of the Patuxent River. Marine life of the Bay is studied at the nearby Chesapeake Biological Laboratory.

The people of Solomons are, for the most part, descended from a group of oyster shuckers brought there from the Eastern Shore about 1870 when a cannery was established on the island by Captain Isaac Solomon. By 1915 when residents awaited the arrival of a steamboat, left, all that remained of the packing plant was a huge pile of oyster shells.

St. Mary's County, like Calvert, is a peninsula. It is bordered by the Patuxent and Potomac rivers and the Chesapeake Bay. Until World War II, when the Navy built a large facility there, the population had been dwindling. In 1940 there were fewer people living in the area than had been there in 1790. St. Mary's is Maryland's oldest county, the site of the landing of the Ark and the Dove, the ships that brought the original colonists, in 1634. Anniversaries have long been celebrated there with style. The group at right was probably participating in a commemoration of the State's 275th birthday.

Above, in 1934 the festivities for the tercentenary were quite elaborate. The pomp, pageantry, and parades included the landing of reproductions of the Ark and the Dove and the opening of the reconstructed first state house at St. Mary's City.

Far right, Andrew Gresko proudly shows off his corn stalks, c. 1930.

Piney Point, on the lower Potomac, was a stylish beach resort between 1820 and 1853. Popular with the political types from Washington, the place became a social center for dignitaries, including President James Monroe, who maintained a cottage that became, in effect, a summer White House. Monroe's home was destroyed by a hurricane in 1933. At right, Susie Combs Burch walked the beach with her children c. 1910.

Other famous visitors to Piney Point included Vice President John C. Calhoun, Secretary of State Henry Clay, the great orator Daniel Webster, and Presidents Franklin Pierce and Theodore Roosevelt. Below, as the steamboat approached the wharf at 1:45 P.M. on July 26, 1908, an expectant crowd prepared to come aboard.

St. Mary's County remains largely rural. In recent years it counted more licensed oystermen than any other community in Maryland. The Redgate Store near Leonardtown, left, served the area around Breton Bay.

Agricultural agents of the University of Maryland Extension Service helped demonstrate how local farmers could fight plant and animal diseases. In 1931 the next generation got a lesson in raising corn right in the field.

The first airplane landed in Leonardtown, the county seat, in 1918. The town was named in honor of Benedict Leonard Calvert, the fourth Lord Baltimore, in 1728. It was raided by the British in the War of 1812.

FOLLOWING PAGES:
Pointed hats were the order of the day at the oxcart races that were part of an oyster roast held at Medley's Neck near Leonardtown, c. 1915. Oxen were used to haul tobacco from neighboring farms to Leonardtown for shipment to Baltimore until World War II.

Butchering time at the Mattingly farm in Leonardtown was a busy time for the entire family. At right, Mrs. Mattingly and her son prepare sausage at the kitchen table.

Lester Mattingly took his responsibility to bring home the bacon quite seriously. He and his helper had cut up the whole hog—and then some—when the photograph below was made.

Far right, Mrs. Mattingly draws lard in an iron kettle over an open fire while her children play on the woodpile.

La Plata is the sprawling seat of government for Charles County. The town came into existence shortly after the arrival of the Pope's Creek railroad in 1868. The original county seat, Port Tobacco, was once a thriving port, but the river there had silted up so much by the end of the nineteenth century that emphasis had shifted to the railroad. In 1891 when the old court house in Port Tobacco burned down a new one was built in La Plata. The width of Charles Street in 1936 appears to have allowed for drivers to establish their own lanes of traffic.

Far left, in the early colonial period the cultivation of tobacco was Maryland's principal commercial activity. Growing the same crop year after year gradually exhausted much good farmland, especially on the Eastern Shore. Only in Southern Maryland is tobacco still grown and cured in large quantities. Each crop takes fifteen months of care, and virtually all the work is done by hand.

There are two Wicomico Rivers in Maryland, one on the Eastern Shore, the other, pictured at left, divides St. Mary's and Charles counties and is a branch of the Potomac. Bushwood Landing, seen here from an approaching steamboat, is on the St. Mary's side of the river.

Like most of Southern Maryland, Charles County has remained largely agricultural. In 1935 the county extension agent demonstrated the use of a portable sheep-dipping vat.

Business seems to have been slow at the La Plata Hotel c. 1910. Indian tribes inhabited much of Charles County long before the first white settlers arrived. For centuries Pope's Creek was a meeting place where the Indians ate oysters. Over the years the heaps of shells came to cover thirty acres, in some places fifteen-feet high.

A pageant entitled "Neighbor Washington: A Portrayal of His Life on the Tidewater Potomac" was presented at the Charles County Fair in 1932.

The wharf at Marshall Hall was loaded with hogsheads of tobacco when the steamboat arrived c. 1910. The Marshall Hall estate, granted to William Marshall in 1690, was developed into an amusement park in the twentieth century.

The Wakefield stopped at Grinder's Wharf near Indian Head on Mattawoman Creek c. 1910.

Southern Maryland was hard hit by the Civil War. Sympathies generally ran with the Confederacy, so the Union army kept careful patrols like this one at Rosecroft Point in September of 1863. It was into Charles County that John Wilkes Booth escaped and hid for a week before crossing into Virginia.

Fort Washington is located on a high bluff overlooking the Potomac River in Prince George's County. The site was selected by George Washington in 1795, but the land was not purchased until 1808. Its location made it an ideal fortification for protecting the new national capital, but the commander balked at the approach of the British in 1814 and never fired a shot.

Far right, the caption on this view at the lighthouse at Fort Washington gives credence to the report that the Potomac River was once a bountiful source of caviar. The men boarding the small craft are identified as "Spawntakers embarking, 1891."

River View Park was a popular amusement park begun by the same Randall family that operated many of the famous steamers on the Potomac.

The engine that powered the merry-go-round at River View Park once supplied steam to a riverboat.

In addition to the rides, the park featured a dance hall, a large open-air restaurant and a bowling alley, all of which made it a favorite excursion place for the young people of nearby Washington, D.C.

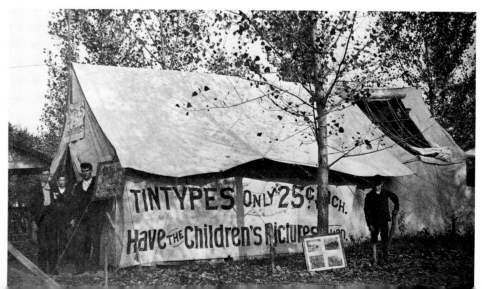

Memories of a pleasant day at the resort c. 1900 could be guaranteed by having pictures made by the tintype photographer.

There wasn't much left on Main Street in Piscataway in 1910: what had once been a prosperous port was left with little importance when the creek filled with silt.

Although there are few descendants left, some traces of Native American heritage remain in Maryland. This family is apparently a blend of black and Indian blood. In 1908, when this photograph was made in Piscataway, the Indians were shunned by most whites and for the most part preferred not to associate with blacks. Consequently an unfortunate degree of marriage among close relatives and many albino offspring resulted.

Mount Lubentia in Largo was built some time before 1770. It was named for the birthplace in Scotland of Ninian Beall who patented the estate in 1696. Two of his descendants, Washington Beall Bowie and Rosalie Beall Bowie, are seen here on the lawn c. 1898.

Upper Marlboro is the Prince George's County seat. The economy of the town and the surrounding area is based on tobacco. In 1938 a major change took place in the marketing of the crop. Prior to that time growers shipped directly to buyers in Baltimore or sold to local factors. When the tobacco auction houses were opened in 1938 a considerable savings was enjoyed by the growers. The Upper Marlboro Academy, left, was a local school c. 1915.

The village of Bowie was at the junction of the main line of the Pennsylvania Railroad and the Pope's Creek Branch. In 1940 it had only a few frame houses, an Odd Fellow's Hall, and some small shops. In modern times it developed into a huge bedroom community for commuters into Washington, D.C.

In 1908 the State of Maryland purchased the Baltimore Normal School and moved it to Bowie. Originally established in 1867, the school was intended as an institution for training Negro teachers. After the move to Bowie, emphasis switched for some years to industrial subjects, but in 1928 it became an accredited four-year college, again specializing in teacher education.

The college maintained an elementary school where student teachers could practice their skills. In 1931 the youngsters were not the only beginners in the classroom.

In 1939, a doctor and nurse checked the physical condition and medical histories of preschoolers at a clinic for potential students at the school affiliated with Bowie State College.

The Maryland suburbs surrounding Washington, D.C., offered comfortable homes and spacious neighborhoods for many bureaucrats employed by the federal government. The Bowling residence in Berwyn, near College Park, was photographed by Robert Sadler on June 6, 1909.

The post office at Berwyn impressed photographer John Vachon twenty-eight years later when he decided to include it with his contributions to the Farm Security Administration photographic survey of the United States.

The Maryland Agricultural College was chartered as a private institution in 1856, one of the first of its kind. In 1914 the State of Maryland assumed control, and in 1920 the University of Maryland in Baltimore merged with the college, making the College Park campus part of the university. The Agricultural Experiment Station building was originally the Rossborough Inn, dated 1798. The livestock show at left was held on May 31, 1924.

The private laboratory of the first state entomologist, Willis G. Johnson, clearly demonstrates the professor's consuming interest: the study of insects. The portrait of the scientist at work was made on June 20, 1899.

The College Park airport was the terminus for the first scheduled air mail service among New York, Philadelphia, and Washington, D.C. The workers at the air mail station posed for the camera c. 1912. The airport closed in 1913.

233

Experiments at the Government Aero Park

from *The Book of the Royal Blue*, October 1909

The experiments of the army aeroplane at College Park, Md., have become a matter of much interest to passengers of the Baltimore & Ohio Railroad between Baltimore and Washington. Wilbur Wright, the instructor, and his pupils, Lieutenants Lahm, Humphries and Foulois, do not select any particular time of the day for their experiments. Sometimes they fly in the early morning and again in the late evening and like as not at mid-day, if the wind is not high. Consequently, there is continued expectancy among the passengers as the trains pass in full view along the entire edge of the field.

Aviation just now is the topic of the world and everybody reads the latest information on the subject. Those of our own country read the daily reports from the Government aviation field, where the Wright machines are in daily practice; consequently, there is hardly a passenger on any of the through trains of the Baltimore & Ohio Railroad between New York, Philadelphia, Baltimore, Washington and Western cities but anticipates a glimpse of the flying machines as his train passes along the Government grounds.

On the other hand, the "every hour" express trains between Baltimore and Washington furnish an equal amount of interest to the aviators, who, on several occasions, have flown their "big bird" alongside of and in the same direction as the fast-moving express, thus establishing additional food for thought as to the possibilities of travel by air.

Mr. Wright made history when he flew from Governor's Island up the Hudson River and around the warships at Spuyten Duyvil and back again, a distance of twenty miles. Mr. Wright has now made more history by flying his machine along the line of the first railroad and the first telegraph. It is over eighty-one years since the railroad was established, and over sixty-five years since the first telegraph message was sent between Baltimore and Washington. The aeroplane is in its infancy and it is safe to predict that there will be greater strides in the evolution of this machine than there were in the perfection of either railroad or telegraph.

For three weeks in October 1909 Wilbur Wright gave lessons in aviation at the U.S. Army Flying School at College Park. One of the favorite experiments for both participants and spectators took place when the pilots raced their machines against commuter trains.

Wright and his students made an average of four or five flights a day, usually early in the morning or late in the evening to avoid attracting crowds.

In 1847 William and Elias Ellicott built an iron furnace at Muirkirk. In 1924 the Mineral Pigments Corporation, successor to the original iron works, began producing dry pigments from foreign ores. It was Christmas Day 1925 when this small band of workers and their children posed in front of company housing.

The Muirkirk Iron Works supplied cannons and cannonballs to the Union army during the Civil War. In 1872, when the photograph below was made, it was providing ore to the Baltimore & Ohio Railroad. In 1880 the plant was destroyed by an explosion, but it was quickly rebuilt.

The George Washington House at Bladensburg was built c. 1755 and was then called the Indian Maid Tavern. Bladensburg was chartered in 1742 and was for a time an important port on the Anacostia River. For a few years it was the terminus of the Baltimore & Ohio Railroad because Congress refused to allow railroads to enter Washington, but that ban was lifted in 1835.

Judging by the tools of their trade, soldiers assigned to kitchen duty at Camp Meade c. 1910 appear to have had all sorts of responsibilities.

Scoutmaster Robert E. Ennis of Capitol Heights had the undivided attention of his troop as he plotted their next adventure.

Although most of northern Prince George's County would soon become densely populated, there were a few cornfields left in 1905.

At the turn of the century, Laurel seemed to have a bright future. Residents had numerous employment opportunities with cotton and grist mills, a foundry, and a shirt factory all located there. By 1911, however, all of these businesses had been abandoned. With the expansion of nearby Camp Meade during World War II, the population and economy again flourished.

Laurel was the home of gifted amateur photographer Robert Sadler. Because he worked for the railroad, Sadler traveled extensively around the state and seemed to have always taken along his camera. Fortunately, he was meticulous in his captioning and record keeping. He even logged in the exposure settings and the time of day at which his photographs were made. Some of his best views were of his hometown, like these made in the summer of 1908. The Treasury streetcar at the electric car station was about to depart for downtown Washington, D.C.

Sadler attended the Emancipation Day parade in Laurel in 1914, held, no doubt, to recall the issuance of the Emancipation Proclamation by President Abraham Lincoln which declared the freedom of all slaves in territory still at war with the Union. It went into effect on January 1, 1863.

Even the new family auto needed a drink once in a while. Fortunately, Father remembered to bring along the watering can in 1914.

WESTERN Maryland

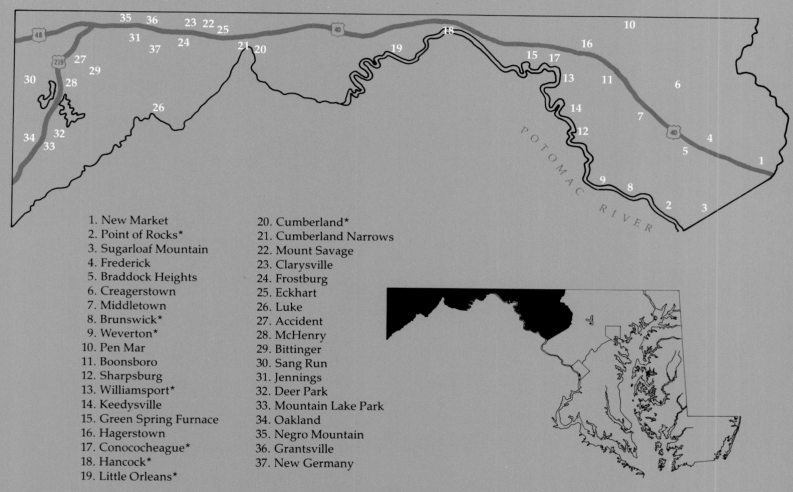

1. New Market
2. Point of Rocks*
3. Sugarloaf Mountain
4. Frederick
5. Braddock Heights
6. Creagerstown
7. Middletown
8. Brunswick*
9. Weverton*
10. Pen Mar
11. Boonsboro
12. Sharpsburg
13. Williamsport*
14. Keedysville
15. Green Spring Furnace
16. Hagerstown
17. Conococheague*
18. Hancock*
19. Little Orleans*

20. Cumberland*
21. Cumberland Narrows
22. Mount Savage
23. Clarysville
24. Frostburg
25. Eckhart
26. Luke
27. Accident
28. McHenry
29. Bittinger
30. Sang Run
31. Jennings
32. Deer Park
33. Mountain Lake Park
34. Oakland
35. Negro Mountain
36. Grantsville
37. New Germany

*On the C & O Canal

Life on the Chesapeake & Ohio Canal is exemplified by this portrait of John McDaniel and his wife standing on the porch of their home just below Little Orleans on September 27, 1896.

Long before New Market became the antiques capital of Maryland, it was a quiet little town on the edge of Frederick County, right on the National Road. Weary travelers were both welcome and well fed at the Utz Hotel, right.

The local physician, Dr. Hopkins, was also an accomplished amateur photographer. Hopkins enjoyed making a visual record of his community, and his friends and neighbors seem to have been equally agreeable to posing for his camera. The two groups shown here, below left and right, represented a cross section of the citizens of New Market and its environs, their modes of dress, and their interests.

When the circus came to New Market, everyone, including Dr. Hopkins, came out to see the elephants.

FOLLOWING PAGES:
Located on the east end of New Market, this homestead illustrates many aspects of rural living in the not-too-distant past: fields plowed by horse, wood as a source of fuel for heating and cooking, the kitchen garden and fruit trees, a smokehouse, laundry hung out to dry in the sun.

The flood of June 1889 caused extensive damage to communities along the Potomac River and to the Chesapeake & Ohio Canal. Point of Rocks was among the towns where the water had risen to dangerously high levels by June 2, above.

By June 5, the community was hard at work cleaning up the damage to buildings and the railroad line, right and far right.

Disaster struck again in 1937 when the Potomac flooded on April 28. When this photograph was taken at 1:00 P.M., the water had already receded five feet.

Excursions into the great outdoors were a favorite pastime for Marylanders. The hearty hikers at right trekked up Sugarloaf Mountain to reach this rocky perch.

The dapper gents pictured below brought many conveniences of home with them on their hunting trip, including wine decanters, china plates, and, apparently, a cook.

Some folks in Frederick County, like these coon hunters, far right, seem to have taken their sport very seriously.

Because it was located right on the National Road, Frederick was a popular stopping point on the route to Cumberland and beyond. This coach stopped at J. Water's shop c. 1880. According to his sign, Mr. Water was a dealer in wool and sheepskins, as well as a manufacturer of neat's foot oil.

Tradition holds that a demijohn of whiskey was sealed into the huge stone jug at the eastern end of the famous Jug Bridge by Leonard Harbough, who constructed the bridge at a cost of $55,000 for the turnpike company in 1807–8. It was here that the Marquis de Lafayette was greeted by the people of Frederick when he visited in 1824. Note that there were flood conditions when the picture at right was made.

Rose Hill Manor was the last home of Maryland's first governor, Thomas Johnson. By 1907, when this picture was made, it was owned by Noel Cramer. In recent years, Rose Hill was restored and converted into a children's museum.

The fountain at Seventh and Market streets greeted travelers approaching Frederick from Gettysburg, Pennsylvania. This photograph was made by Jacob Byerly, one of Frederick's first photographers, who died about 1881. Both his son, John Davis Byerly, and his grandson, Charles Byerly, pursued the same profession.

One of Frederick's firefighters was willing to go to great heights to welcome his colleagues from the rest of Maryland and Delaware, far right.

254

The poignant caption on the reverse of the photograph far left, "My family as it was for a time last summer," is a bittersweet reminder that change is inevitable.

Francis Scott Key practiced law in Frederick for some time after 1800. To honor the one-time resident, the people of Frederick erected a monument to Key's memory, left.

The building for the Emergency Hospital of Frederick County, below, was purchased and occupied in November 1903. It was located on South Market Street.

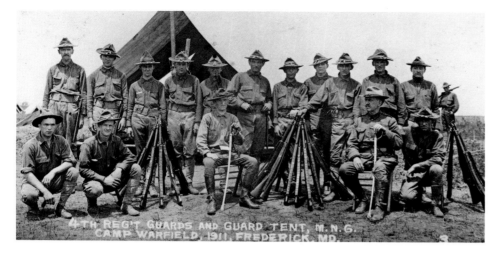

A streetcar stops at Square Corner on a busy day in downtown Frederick, far left. At the turn of the century a trolley line was laid to Middletown Valley; it was later extended to Hagerstown.

In 1911, the Fourth Regiment of the Maryland National Guard assembled at Camp Warfield in Frederick.

This view of the swinging bridge for pedestrians on Bentz Street in Frederick became a classic turn-of-the-century picture post card. The town mill on the left was torn down in 1926; Baker Park took its place.

J. E. Price & Co. Agricultural House at Square Corner, left (seen on the right in the photograph far left) sold every sort of implement to local farmers, including McCormick harvesting machines and Studebaker wagons.

The Woman's College, founded in Frederick in 1893, became Hood College in 1912 to honor Margaret Scholl Hood, a "generous friend" of the college. Mrs. Hood was an alumna of the Frederick Female Seminary, which had formerly occupied the buildings of the college. At right, students conduct experiments in the chemistry laboratory.

The Maryland School for the Deaf, below and opposite page, was located on Market Street in Frederick. Students were trained in academic subjects, calisthenics, and trades such as shoe repairing, printing, cabinetmaking, and domestic science.

Far left, the lazy days of summer lured many a young boy to a good fishing spot on a quiet stream.

The older boys were bustling in October 1909 at the Frederick County Fair, perhaps getting ready for a horse race, left.

Hilda Cushwa of Clear Spring still remembers the day she, her parents, and Mildred Adams paused in Braddock Heights to have their picture taken—a welcome break in a long auto trip to Baltimore, below.

The old stone mill, above, was typical of several such structures in Frederick County.

The members of the Monocacy Reformed Church in Creagerstown came out in their Sunday best to celebrate the church's 190th anniversary in 1922, right.

WELCOME
To The 175th Anniversary Of The Organization
Of The Old Monocacy Reformed Church.
And
The 190th Anniversary Of The Building Of
The Old Monocacy Log Church.
Ma   1922

SITE OF OLD
MONOCACY
LOG CHURCH
BUILT 1732

Weverton, on the Baltimore & Ohio Railroad, is the first town encountered in Washington County after leaving Frederick County. The depot, left, seems to have been a meeting place for men only.

In the autumn of 1898, Admiral Winfield Scott Schley, a native of Frederick, visited Middletown with his family and well-wishers, below. That same year Admiral Schley became a national hero and a source of official controversy when he destroyed the Spanish fleet at Santiago during the Spanish-American War.

Brunswick Revisited

BY RUSSELL BAKER

from *Growing Up*, 1982

*B*runswick was a huge railway center on the B&O Main Line, which linked the Atlantic coast to Chicago and midwestern steel centers. Approaching it was almost unbearably thrilling. You crossed an endless, rickety cantilever bridge after pausing on the Virginia bank to pay a one-dollar toll. This was a powerful sum of money, but Brunswick was not for the pinchpennies of the earth. As you neared the far end of the bridge, its loose board floor rattling under the car wheels, the spectacle unfolding before you made the dollar seem well spent.

In the foreground lay a marvelous confusion of steel rails, and in the midst of them, on a vast cinder-covered plain, the great brick roundhouse with its doors agape, revealing the snouts of locomotives undergoing surgery within. Smaller yard locomotives chugged backward and forward, clacking boxcar couplings together and sending up infernos of black gritty smoke which settled over the valley in layers.

If the crossing gate was down, you might be treated to the incredible spectacle of a passenger express highballing toward glory, the engineer waving down at you from the cab window, sparks flying, cinders scattering, the glistening pistons pumping with terrifying power. And behind this hellish monstrosity throbbing with fire and steam, a glimpse of the passengers' faces stately and remote as kings as they roared by in a gale of wind powerful enough to knock you almost off your feet.

Between the mountains that cradled the yard there seemed to be thousands of freight cars stretching back so far toward Harpers Ferry that you could never see the end of them. And flanking the tracks on the far side, a metropolis: Brunswick had electric light bulbs, telephones, radios. Rich people lived there. Masons, for heaven's sake. Not just Red Men and Odd Fellows and Moose such as we had around Morrisonville, but Masons. And not just Masons, but Baptists, too—genuine dress-to-the-teeth-and-give-yourself-fancy-airs Baptists.

Three of my uncles lived there: Uncle Tom, Uncle Harvey, and Uncle Lewis. They were expected to come back to Morrisonville and sit on Ida Rebecca's porch too, but only on Sundays. As citizens of Brunswick, they had crossed over into a world of Byzantine splendor.

Brunswick had a department store and a movie house. There was a street stretching for two or three blocks lined with stores, including a drugstore where you could sit down at a round marble-top table and have somebody bring you an ice-cream soda. There were whole blocks of houses jammed right up against another, the blocks laid out in a grid pattern on hills steep enough to tire a mountain goat.

Uncle Harvey lived with his wife and daughter at the crest of one such hill. He was one of God's favored people, a locomotive engineer. I was in terror that he might try to engage me in conversation. When he heard a train whistle echoing off the valley below, I goggled in admiration as he produced his big railroad watch, studied it coolly, and announced, "The three-fifty-four's running five minutes late today."

My Uncle Tom worked as a blacksmith in the B&O yards near Harpers Ferry. That was a good job too. Though he walked the four-mile round trip to and from the shop daily in sooty railroader's clothes, Uncle Tom was well off. His house contained a marvel I had never seen before: an indoor bathroom. This was enough to mark Uncle Tom a rich man, but in addition he had a car. And such a car. It was an Essex, with windows that rolled up and down with interior hand cranks, not like my father's Model T with the isinglass windows in side curtains that had to be buttoned onto the frame in bad weather. Uncle Tom's Essex even had cut-glass flower vases in sconces in the backseat. He was a man of substance. When he rolled up in his Essex for Ida Rebecca's command appearances on Sunday afternoons in Morrisonville, wearing a white shirt and black suit, smoking his pipe, his pretty red-haired wife Goldie on the seat beside him, I felt pride in kinship to so much grandeur.

Lewis, Ida Rebecca's youngest son, also thrived in Brunswick, at the barbering trade. Though scarcely twenty-five years old, he had his own shop and called by appointment on the Brunswick ladies to cut their hair at home in the new boyish bobs and sometimes, according to people envious of Uncle Lewis's reputation for gallantry, to render more knightly service. Uncle Lewis was my first vision of what male elegance could be. He had glistening black hair always parted so meticulously that you might have thought he needed surveyor's instruments to comb a line so straight. Thin black sideburns extended down to his earlobes in the style cartoonists adopted as the distinguishing mark of high-toned cads. With a high gloss on his city shoes, in his crisp white barber's smock, he wisecracked with the railroad men as he presided in front of a long wall

of mirrors lined with pomades, tonics, and scents. I admired him as the ultimate in dandyism.

On those magic occasions when my father took me to Brunswick, the supreme delight was to have Uncle Lewis seat me on a board placed across the arms of his barber chair, crank me into the sky, and subject me to the pampered luxury of being clippered, snipped, and doused with heavy applications of Lucky Tiger or Jeris hair tonic, which left my hair plastered gorgeously to the sides of my head and sent me into the street reeking of aromatic delight.

After one such clipping I climbed a hill in Brunswick with my father to call at Uncle Tom's house. Though Uncle Tom was fourteen years older, my father loved and respected him above all his brothers. Maybe it was because he saw in Tom the blacksmith some shadow of the blacksmith father who died when my father was only ten. Maybe it was because Tom,

Located on the Potomac River, Brunswick was once a bustling railroad town with a roundhouse similar to the one pictured here as its focal point. The caption on this stereoscopic view, published by the B & O Railroad, is simply "Western Maryland Roundhouse."

living in such splendor with his indoor bathroom and his Essex, had escaped Morrisonville and prospered. Maybe it was for Tom's sweetness of character, which was unusual among Ida Rebecca's boys.

Uncle Tom was at work that day, but Aunt Goldie gave us a warm welcome. She was a delicate woman, not much bigger than my mother, with hair of ginger red, blue eyes, and a way of looking at you and turning her head suddenly this way and that which reminded me of an alert bird. She was also a notoriously fussy housekeeper, constantly battling railroad grime to preserve her house's reputation for not containing "a speck of dust anywhere in it." Before admitting us to her spotless kitchen, she had my father and me wipe our shoes on the doormat, then made a fuss about how sweet I smelled and how handsome I looked, then cut me a huge slab of pie.

My great joy in calling on Aunt Goldie was the opportunity afforded to visit the indoor bathroom, so naturally after polishing off the pie I pretended an urgent need to use the toilet. This was on the second floor and required a journey through the famously dust-free dining room and parlor, but Aunt Goldie understood. "Take your shoes off first so you don't track up the floor," she said. Which I did. "And don't touch anything in the parlor."

With this caution she admitted me to the sanctum of spotlessness. I trod across immaculate rugs and past dining room furniture, armchairs, side tables, a settee, like a soldier walking in a mine field. There would be no dust left behind if I could help it.

At the top of the stairs lay the miracle of plumbing. Shutting the door to be absolutely alone with it, I ran my fingers along the smooth enamel of the bathtub and glistening faucet handles of the sink. The white majesty of the toilet bowl, through which gallons of water could be sent rushing by the slightest touch of a silvery lever, filled me with envy. A roll of delicate paper was placed beside it. Here was luxury almost too rich to be borne by anyone whose idea of fancy toiletry was Uncle Irvey's two-hole privy and a Montgomery Ward catalog.

After gazing upon it as long as I dared without risking interruption by a search party, I pushed the lever and savored the supreme moment when thundering waters emptied into the bowl and vanished with a mighty gurgle. It was the perfect conclusion to a trip to Brunswick.

The High Rock Observatory, near Pen Mar, was built in 1878. The view above, taken in 1903 by the Detroit Publishing Company for one of its famous post cards, takes in an area purported to be two thousand square miles.

The Western Maryland Railway provided excellent service to the resort at Pen Mar. John Mifflen Hood, president of the railroad, first established the amusement park high atop the Blue Ridge Mountains on the border between Pennsylvania and Maryland in 1877.

The Blue Mountain House, built in 1883, was the most elegant of the many hotels in the vicinity of Pen Mar. In its heyday it boasted 300 rooms—each with a telephone—a post office, a chapel, bowling alleys, tennis courts, billiards rooms, stables, and a ballroom.

The hotel was lost to fire on August 5, 1913, when more than two hundred guests and fifty staff members were asleep. There was no loss of life, but the hotel, valued at more than $300,000, was never rebuilt.

The amusement park at Pen Mar had many attractions, but the most popular was the miniature railroad. The first train was purchased in 1904; another was acquired from the Jamestown Exposition.

The crowds at Pen Mar came from far and near.
There were excursionists picnicking for the day,
vacationers, and the wealthy who owned summer
cottages in the woods. Senators and ambassadors
journeyed from Washington, D.C., while business executives bustled up from Baltimore for a
respite from the city's heat.

Unfortunately, the road into Pen Mar Park was
also the road out, and every happy excursion
eventually came to an end. With the increase of
automobile travel, railroad resorts like Pen Mar
lost their appeal. The resort, which had been in
decline since the fire at the Blue Mountain House
in 1913, closed permanently in 1943.

268

PRECEDING PAGES:
It had been a good day of picking when C. D. Young stopped by Joe Brown's orchard and berry patch to capture this candid portrait of the farmer and his family at work. Boonsboro was fortunate to have the sensitive eye of Young, a local photographer, observing its life styles and activities.

On a sunny day in 1910, Jennie Witter gave this charming tea party, which Young attended.

It was a big day in town when Dr. S. S. Davis bought his brand-new Ford. His was the first automobile in Boonsboro; he soon hired a chauffeur to crank it up—and to drive it, too, of course.

272

Josh Flock and his wife posed for Young's camera c. 1910.

Boonsboro went to great lengths with this red-white-and-blue parade to celebrate some big event, perhaps the return of its native sons from Mexico or World War I, c. 1917–19.

On July 24, 1827, the people of Boonsboro climbed nearby South Mountain to construct a monument to the memory of George Washington. Fifty-four feet in circumference at its base, the structure was composed of stones laid without mortar. Not surprisingly, by 1927 it had all but completely tumbled down. In 1935 it was rebuilt by Civilian Conservation Corps workers, left.

273

Antietam: An Eyewitness Account

BY OTHO NESBITT

The following are excerpts selected from the diary of Otho Nesbitt of Clear Spring. These entries were written just before and after the battle of Antietam in September, 1862. They are reprinted here with kind permission of Nesbitt's granddaughters, Mrs. Lillie Fiery, Mrs. Nora Snyder and Mrs. Florence Frantz.

Sept. 5

Clear Spring is full of refugees again from Virginia. Our armies all driven into Washington. Various rumors afloat; one that they are crossing at Edward's Ferry, Leesburg, and other places. 'Tis reported they are in Frederick. Commissary stores burnt in Frederick City.

Sept. 7

Town full of refugees. Gen. Kearney sent a picket into a wood to see if there were any Rebels there. Came back and reported no one present. Not being satisfied, went out himself and was shot. His body sent in next morning with a flag of truce.

Sept. 8

Rebels in and about Frederick in force—100 or 120,000. All kinds of reports of late. Bradley Johnston, Provost Marshall of the city, said the Rebels have a tremendous army. One paper says by summing up the amount of all—260,000 infantry and 20,000 horses.

Sept. 10

This is a day long to be remembered. Ever since 12 o'clock last night, they have been

Antietam Creek could be viewed clearly from the vantage point of Elk Mountain. Union signalmen watched from here as Lee's army moved about part of the three-mile-long battlefield. The tower was built after the conflict in September 1862. These images of Antietam were made by noted photographers Timothy O'Sullivan and Alexander Gardner.

Otho Nesbitt, author of the diary

going. First they came from Williamsport: horses, mules, men, and machines. Then the news about 11 or 12 o'clock came they were in Hagerstown and Williamsport. No mistake. The excitement which had been kept up all morning began to run high. And about 12 or 1 o'clock everything put for the mountain, and there are scarcely anything left but women and children. Isaac (Nesbitt) and Bill Dellinger about 2 o'clock took a farewell home with me and left for Mercersburg. Not withstanding the long drought, the day is cloudy and drizzling; probably will be a bad night to sleep in the mountain. Harry Miles went along.

Sept. 12

Morris came down out of the mountain and went to work. I went to Hagerstown to see the Rebel army come into Hagerstown. They were a hard drab-colored set—long, lanky, and tawny. I saw Gen. Toombs.

Sept. 14

Heard cannonading nearly all day at Harpers Ferry on the Maryland Heights.

Sept. 15

Heard cannonading apparently from or near Harpers Ferry along the top of the South Mountain for 3 or 4 miles from daylight till after sun-up. It was brisk cannonading.

Sept. 16

'Tis said a great battle has been fought from Middletown to the top of the South Mountain, and the Rebels are making their way across the river as fast as they can. Many are going from the Clear Spring this morning to see the battlefield. It was fought on Saturday and Sunday and Monday. 'Tis said they have lost 30,000 killed and wounded.

Sept. 17

Many who went down from Clear Spring say the Rebel dead on top of the mountain didn't amount to more than 200. They were still lying there all swelled up and black in the face—something very bad. They were buried today. Harpers Ferry on the Maryland Heights was taken on Monday and 7 or 8 thousand surrendered and are prisoners of war. A tremendous battle has been going on today from daylight till dark near Sharpsburg, Keedysville, and Bakersville. The cannons and musketry have been roaring all day.

Sept. 18

Went down to the battle field at Sharpsburg today and saw part of it. 'Tis said it was 5 or 6 or 7 miles long and from 1 to 1½ miles or 2 broad. Rode over a portion of the battle field on the right wing. Saw about 50 dead horses and probably 50 dead men whom they were burying . . . Union men. Left the group awhile before night and went to the crossroads some 4 or 5 miles on the Sharpsburg Pike from the camp towards Hagerstown. There a young trooper had a notion to press my horse. I asked to stay at the tavern all night, but the landlord told me he was

The battle of Antietam, also known as Sharpsburg, was the bloodiest single day of fighting during the Civil War and the only conflict to be waged on Maryland soil. Combined losses numbered more than twenty-three thousand men killed or wounded. Above, note the corpses strewn around the field and the soldier on the left, who was black.

full of officers and men and recommended me to go up on the hill to a farm house where a William Wolf lived . . . a very clever man. I did and got to stay all night. Whilst there 2 fellows from Pennsylvania and 2 from Virginia came in and wanted to stay all night, and after permission, we all got supper and talked till 10 or 11 o'clock. Next morning the 2 horsemen and myself started for camp, one of them giving me a description of the man-

ner how he saw them taking off legs and arms at the hospital. First they chloroformed them. One boy complained very much that they would smother him. He had an arm to be taken off. He also saw the leg above the knee taken off a large man. They first cut the flesh around where they intended to cut it off and then took up the arteries and tied the ends of them. Then shoved the flesh up the bone 3 or 4 inches, and then sawed it off. Drew the flesh back. Closed it together, and the job was done. I heard a fellow say passing by one hospital he saw quite a pile of legs and arms lying nearby. Down in the clover field I saw a leg with the shoe and stocking on. Was taken off just below the knee about half way down. I saw two hospitals with about 40 in each. Others said they saw one with 900 and upwards in a house and barn . . . all Union men. Probably 1,000 killed and 3, 4, or 5,000

wounded on each side. The whole country around about is a hospital. Houses and barns full.

Sept. 19
Went on the battle field again and was permitted to go where I pleased. The Union men were nearly all buried; the army in motion. Two columns appeared to go towards the river about a mile apart, and the balance went down the Sharpsburg Pike . . . a mighty host. 'Tis said McClellan has probably 200 or 250,000 and the other side not much less. I rode on to the battle field where the Rebels formed their line of battle. They were not buried. I could see their line distinctly by the dead lying along it as they fell. Nearly all lying on their backs as if they hadn't even made a struggle. The line I suppose was a mile long or more. I could sit on my horse and count 50 dead

Few historians doubt that had General McClellan and his far larger army challenged General Lee to another day of fighting at Antietam, the war might have ended then. Instead, McClellan planned strategy while Lee and his troops slipped into Virginia. On October 3, President Lincoln came to Sharpsburg to urge pursuit. When McClellan refused, he was relieved of his command.

On September 16, 1862, the Confederate cavalry captured the stone bridge over Antietam Creek, on the turnpike between Sharpsburg and Boonsboro. This tranquil scene shows but few traces of the bitter fighting that had taken place here a few days earlier, though the overturned stone wall on the far side gives a clue.

On September 17, 1880, Miss Helen Wright, daughter of General G. B. Wright of Ohio, drew the veil from the U. S. Soldier Monument at Antietam National Cemetery. The statue weighed thirty tons and took more than four years to carve. Before its official dedication, it was displayed in Philadelphia at the entrance to the Centennial exhibitions in 1876–77.

General and Mrs. McClellan stayed for several weeks at the home of a Mrs. Lee, at right, after the battle. Although Lincoln issued the Emancipation Proclamation on September 23, the woman on the left was not set free as a result. His edict concerned slaves in the seceded states only; Maryland was officially neutral.

men. Just around about. On the side 100 yards further I could do nearly the same. Along the turnpike and the fences on each side they were lying thick. They fell all over the fields more or less as they retreated. I saw where a cannon had been placed and the powder wagon there where a ball had gone through. And there lay 2 horses and 9 men as if the thunder had struck them. A soldier picked up a piece of shell and showed me and said probably the bursting of that shell might have done the whole business. Near the pike I saw a white bull or steer lying on his back all swelled up and 2 sheep nearby all swelled up ready to burst. Down in the corn field I saw a man with a hole in his belly about as big as a hat and about a quart of dark-looking maggots working away. They were all swelled up and black and purple in their faces. I saw Samuel Mumma's fine brick house and barn that was burnt and a small stable close by with a dead horse in that had busted the door half way open as he fell. Another barn was burnt close by, 4 or 5 small houses, and stables in Sharpsburg. At another farm house I saw a steer dead in the yard and a horse dead at the end of the barn just outside and 2 gray horses in the lane just below. In the barnyard were hay stacks and a thrashing machine. I saw them burying their dead, some in single graves and some in trenches. Officers were all buried in single graves. The men were brought to the place of burying and laid on their backs on the ground and their names were written on a piece of paper and the regiment and company they belonged to and laid on their breast or stuck under their fallis or pinned on a blanket thrown over them till the grave or trench was ready and then put in. In the trench probably crossways and a half inch board at the head and foot of each one of them was placed the name, regiment and company. The Rebels were put in a trench and a board put at one end with the number put on. I saw probably 500 dead and from what others said didn't see more than half the battle field for some said it extended far below Sharpsburg. I left about 12 o'clock for home, having satisfied myself in regard to falling humanity. Coming into the Sharpsburg Pike from a hospital not far off, I met Johnston, Joe Boyd, Isaiah Boward, and others going home at the mouth of the road leading through Bakersville and Downsville to Williamsport. As we went up that road we met

On September 22, 1862—six days after the battle of Antietam—blacksmiths were busily working at the forge in Sharpsburg, where General McClellan's headquarters was then located. Much of their work was shoeing horses brought in to replace the hundreds killed in the fighting.

The enormous statue that memorializes the soldiers lost at Antietam was carved by James Pollette. He was twenty-six years old when the work was completed. Pollette followed a design conceived by George Keller, possibly the gentleman pictured above to give a sense of the immensity of the figure.

Russell's troop coming down at a pretty fast gait. Afterwards a good many companies of horses going to Williamsport. We came up to a few houses when we saw Isaiah Boward on the ground. Said they had taken his horse. Joe Boyd told him he would have to submit to it. They would give him a certificate. Johnston and I put out as fast as we could for fear they would attract our horses. After riding some distance, one rode up along side of me and said I expect we shall have to exchange bridles stating his circle was broken and he couldn't hold his horse. I told him my bridle would be no better as it had no circle on. I asked him if he had any regular authority for pressing things.

He said that here comes an officer and that I should ask him. Stating the case to the officer, he told him he ought not to press anything unless it was in the neighborhood. So I rode on till I got to Downsville, seeing 10 or 15 citizens coming back. Said the Rebels had crossed over the river to Williamsport, and their pickets were not more than a mile ahead. I started with some others in the mouth of another road that ran parallel with the Williamsport and Hagerstown Pike when I saw a trooper coming down it as fast as his horse could run. He said the Rebel pickets were thick along that road not more than a mile back. I put down the Sharpsburg Road some distance and turned to the left into a large woods. I was going some distance when I came to a spot of bluegrass in an opening in the woods where I let my horse eat awhile. I then mounted and made on till I came to an open country where there was a fine lot of large peach trees along a lane and some fine ones lying on the ground. I went over and ate a lot of them. Then two men came riding up. Driven back as I was, we all three rode to a fine farm house close by where we stated our case and asked to stay all night . . . which was granted. We rode to the front of the house and hitched our horses, and going in the gate, there sat a half bushel basket full of nice peaches. Being asked to eat some, we did. So when two other men came, driven back and wanting to stay all night, we all went up to the house and sat on the porch awhile. Went to the back part of the house where there was a fountain, took a wash, and ate supper. Then we sat and chatted awhile. When a waiter of fine peaches came in, we ate them. Then in came a waiter of pears. We ate a portion of them, sat a while, and feeling ourselves uncomfortably full, we went to bed.

The purpose of the Chesapeake & Ohio Canal was to carry coal downstream from Cumberland; occasionally canal boats would transport other goods. Darby Mill, right, was located in Williamsport, the midpoint on the canal, which ran parallel to the Potomac River.

Forty years before the tranquil view below of Main Street, Keedysville, was taken, Confederate and Union troops stormed through on their way to the battlefield at Antietam, just two miles away.

The old mill above was located at Green Spring Furnace, west of Clear Spring, near Fort Frederick.

The Darby Coal Company was also located in Williamsport. From there, coal could easily be loaded onto canal boats.

Hagerstown, the Washington County seat, was once a flourishing rail center, the "Hub City" of Maryland. In 1867 the Baltimore & Ohio Railroad laid a connecting spur from its main line at Weverton; seven years later the distance to Baltimore was cut by twenty miles when the Western Maryland Railway track made a more direct link. In 1880 the Shenandoah Valley Railroad established service to the South. By 1909 the office of the county clerk, right, located in the courthouse, was already well stocked with voluminous records.

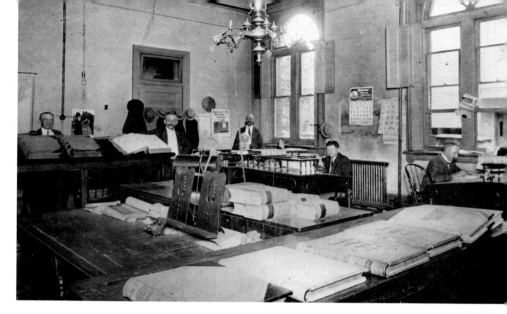

Before the start of the state bicycle meet on July 4, 1889, contenders posed for the camera in the public square in Hagerstown.

Dr. and Mrs. Victor Miller and their wedding party paused for the photographer before the couple boarded a train at the B & O railroad station for their honeymoon trip, June 1, 1905. The Millers' home became the headquarters of the Washington County Historical Society.

Below, in 1917 troops departed from Hagerstown to join Blackjack Pershing in his efforts to guard the Mexican border against raids led by Pancho Villa.

The fire at the railroad car barn at the corner of Summit Avenue and Howard Street on September 10, 1914, completely destroyed the facility.

FOLLOWING PAGES:
Crossing Jonathan Street at West Washington Street seems to have been the thing to do on this day in June 1917. By then, Hagerstown was the third largest city in Maryland. Between 1890 and 1900, the population increased more rapidly than it had during the entire preceding century.

Pleasure Seekers

from a newspaper clipping, August 31, 1894

*I*n response to invitations extended by the Frantz family, of Laurel Hill, near Clear Spring, Md., a number of young persons from the north and east assembled at McCoy's Ferry on Thursday morning, August 23rd, to accompany them on a three days' excursion up the Chesapeake and Ohio canal.

Nearly all who expected to join the party were at the ferry by eight o'clock, and after spending one hour in decorating the "Rudder Grange" with bunting, large and small flags, stretching an awning over the boat, stowing away three days' rations, a two-horse load of melons, our satchels, etc., the call "All Aboard" was given by Captain Bud Castle; Slicky (Alias Will Bowers),

Excursions on the Chesapeake & Ohio Canal were popular even while the waterway was operating commercially. This group from Cumberland posed for photographer Hervey Laney, c. 1890.

cracked his whip, and the mate, W. H. Patton, steered us off from shore amid the waving of handkerchiefs and shouts of good time of those who accompanied us to the ferry.

Our first stop after leaving the ferry was made at old "Fort Frederick," about five miles northeast of Hancock, Md. This historic old fort, about which the reading public know so little, covers one and a half acres of ground and was built by orders of Governor Sharpe in 1755. It is right along the route taken by Braddock on his fatal expedition against Fort Duquesne, and was built to protect the settlers in that section of the State against the marauding Indians who were following the retreating regulars.

During the Civil War several heavy guns were stationed there and since that time Mr. Williams, a Negro, has owned the land surrounding it, and the fort was much neglected, the wells were all filled and the land planted in grapes. But of late years pleasure seekers, relic hunters and those in search of historic data have visited it so frequently that it has been converted into a picnic ground. A pavilion has been erected within the enclosure, and where a century ago men slept with their guns by their sides and ammunition under their pillows to guard against the surprises of hostile Indians, now is heard the jolly, rollicking fun of the picnic party or the *sole*-inspiring music so essential to the tripping of the light fantastic.

After all had secured relics of the fort we resumed our journey up the canal through the Big Pool, so noted for bass and eels, past old Millstone, through the Little Pool, and stopped at Hancock, where we were joined by the remainder of our party. All who had not already seen the widely known town were surprised to find it so small.

After spending forty minutes in the town and meeting many of her sons and fair daughters, we again started on our journey, but soon the scenery changed. No longer did we see such blue mountains in the distance as surrounded old Cumberland Valley.

Mountaintop after mountaintop kept rising higher, rock upon rock kept presenting itself to view, until such magnificent, massive heaps and almost perpendicular walls had been reared that the greatest stretches of our imagination had been surpassed and we were filled with wonder and amazement.

We tied up at 9 P.M. on Thursday night at Hanging Rock, and moved off Friday at 4 A.M., with all aboard asleep. We continued our upward journey until one o'clock, passing through Little Orleans and having changing scenery all the day.

By times we were at the foot of perpendicular rocks from two to three hundred feet high; again we could see to great distances into caverns on the mountain sides which were covered with beds of morning glory, primrose, bouncing bet and other beautiful flowers.

At one P.M. we arrived at the Paw-paw tunnel. It is a grand piece of masonry, and to make the aperture through the mountain of solid slate rock, at the time the canal was made, was considered a great achievement in civil engineering. The arch is made of brick, the wall being the thickness of five lengths of brick or nearly fifty inches. At the top of the arch are found numbers of stalactites, many of which were broken off by members of our party.

These young women enjoyed a pleasant outing on the C & O Canal near Little Orleans in 1896.

We had in our party persons who had climbed Pike's Peak and the Rockies, who wandered through the Adirondacks and the Catskills, who saw Yosemite Valley and the Cañons of the Colorado, who wandered through Yellowstone Park, and sunny Florida, and they united in saying that the scenery of the historic Old Potomac is not excelled.

On Saturday evening, after having taken a bath at the foot of Great Pool, and parted with the chaperon and her son at Cherry Run, we reached the ferry at sunset, were greeted by our friends, and took carriages for Clear Spring.

In spite of its name, the C & O Canal never reached the Ohio, terminating, instead, in Cumberland. Always in competition with the railroad, over the years the canal suffered considerable damage from storms and was often in disrepair.

Thus ended the excursion, but before getting off the boat, cheers and thanks and the yell were given our efficient chaperon and the crew. Arrangements were made to go next summer all along the canal from Cumberland to Georgetown.

The great ''Johnstown'' flood of June 1, 1889, caused extensive damage to the C & O Canal and engulfed communities near the Potomac River. At Conococheague, west of Williamsport, the Western Maryland Railway depot was under water for several days.

By June 5, below, the Western Maryland Railway depot at Conococheague had emerged from the flooded Potomac River.

In its heyday, the C & O Canal carried many boats like this one from Cumberland to Georgetown, with the boats traveling at a rate of two to three miles an hour. Coal was the primary cargo. These scenes, taken at Hancock c. 1900, are typical of many locations along the canal.

Mules were used all along the canal to pull the heavy-laden barges. The great flood of 1924 finally destroyed so much of the canal that it could no longer be used commercially.

289

The photograph above illustrates several aspects of the operation of the locks along the C & O Canal. As the barge passes through the lock, water is diverted into the flume on the right. The lock keeper is seen on the stone wall under the willow tree. His wife is standing on the porch of their home on the left.

The relationship between the C & O Canal and the Potomac River can be seen clearly at right. The canal was constructed well above the river, but floodwaters occasionally rose above the level of the canal.

When Judge Richard A. Kennedy vacationed on the C & O Canal near Little Orleans in 1896, he captured many charming scenes with his camera, like the one at left.

A hunting party along the Potomac paused to record its success, below.

Cumberland, once Maryland's second largest city, is located in a valley formed by the Potomac River. In 1868, and for many years thereafter, Baltimore Avenue, above, was the primary approach from the east.

The stones that paved Baltimore and Mechanic streets in 1857 were undoubtedly an improvement over rutted and muddy dirt roads, but travel on them was still bumpy at best.

Cumberland in 1872, left, was a thriving city, due mainly to its pivotal location in the transportation systems of the time. It was, at once, a railroad center (note the roundhouse at right), the terminus of the C & O Canal, and a site on the National Road.

Captain Boynton's grand aquatic carnival must have had considerable and impressive advance publicity to draw such a devoted crowd on a rainy day in 1891. Reports suggest that those who came to see a man walking on the river and reenactments of famous naval battles may have been disappointed by the day's events.

A favorite winter sport for Cumberland residents was skating on the frozen Potomac River. Note that an ice hockey game was underway when the photograph at right was made.

The ascension of a hot air balloon in 1889 attracted a large number of onlookers to Williams and Park streets where the Baltimore & Ohio Railroad yards were located.

Winter in Western Maryland is often more severe and prolonged than in the rest of the state. For those who enjoy snow and ice, like these children sledding on Washington Street, the colder months are no hardship.

By 1891 Baltimore Street had become congested with signs and symbols of economic prosperity.

Cumberland's streetcar line began operating in 1891, adding more tracks to a city already webbed with railroad lines.

295

A nationwide depression in 1893 inspired five hundred unemployed workers to march from Massilon, Ohio, to Washington, D.C.; they demanded that Congress set up public works programs to create jobs. Led by Jacob Sechler Coxey, the entourage became known as Coxey's Army. They traveled the National Road until they reached Cumberland on Sunday, April 15, 1894. By then a large contingent of newspaper reporters, right, had joined the group, and a media event was in progress.

Coxey's movement had a distinctly religious tone and called itself the Army of the Commonweal of Christ. Carl Browne, Coxey's son-in-law and the most effective organizer and orator of the group, thought that their movement was the prelude to the second coming of Christ. "I believe," Browne wrote, "in the prophecy that He is to come, not in any single form, but in the whole people."

The army never amounted to more than a few hundred men, although they caught the imagination of thousands along their route. To raise badly needed funds, Coxey charged visitors to their camp in Cumberland an admission fee of ten cents. In just two days' time $145 was collected.

Coxey's Army camped at the baseball park for two days. A souvenir pamphlet published to commemorate the event attests that "a more orderly set of men never came to our city, and while tired and dusty, were all in perfectly good humor, though having passed an intensely cold and disagreeable week before." On Tuesday, in an unsuccessful attempt to escape from the press, the army rented two coal barges for $85 and continued the next ninety miles of their journey on the C & O Canal. They disembarked at Williamsport and continued on foot to Washington via Hagerstown, where they rested another three days.

297

Jousting, the official state sport, has attracted competitors and spectators from around the state for many years. The tournament at right was held at the South Cumberland race track in 1895.

Parades have always been crowd pleasers. Here the celebrants were literally hanging out of windows to get a good view of the pageantry.

FANCY WORK BOOTH
EASTERN STAR LAWN CARNIVAL.
CUMBERLAND, MD.

More than a dozen souvenir post-card views remain to stir memories of the Eastern Star Lawn Carnival of July 1909, left and far below. The fancy-work booth featured embroidery, appliqué, dolls, baskets, and parasols.

Narrows Park, above, located on U.S. Route 40 in La Vale, was owned and operated by the street-car company.

SOFT DRINK STAND

The soft-drink stand at the Eastern Star Lawn Carnival seems to have had more than its share of lovely ladies to serve refreshments.

At many locations along the Chesapeake & Ohio Canal, tipples were situated so that coal could be easily loaded onto canal boats. The Cumberland and Pennsylvania Railroad tracks were adjacent to the waterway in Cumberland, right and below.

Cumberland was the end of the line for the C & O Canal. Below, in a section known locally as shantytown, coal was loaded onto canal barges for shipment to Washington, D.C.

Cumberland offered many employment opportunities for the able-bodied like the workers at the Damwell Sawmill, above.

Old German Brewing Company was one of several breweries in Cumberland. Operations there got under way c. 1900.

301

This view of residential Decatur Street clearly illustrates the city's hilly topography.

Hervey Laney is remembered in Cumberland not only as the druggist and proprietor of Laney's Red Lion Pharmacy at 22 North Centre Street, but also as an accomplished photographer. Laney offered the results of his camera artistry for sale at the pharmacy, seen in both photographs below. Hundreds of his original glass-plate negatives have survived: his images are well represented on these pages.

"Celebrities" of all sorts would come to Laney's to be photographed, including a gentleman who planned to walk for a year at a rate of ten miles per day, below left. By the time he reached Cumberland he had traveled 1,650 miles.

Robert Shearer provided a dramatic display for his leather goods store by mounting a large trunk on a pole on Baltimore Street, right.

In August 1921, Cumberland's black baseball team, the Cubs, posed for a group portrait.

For many years Cumberland's competitors have been among the winners at the National Marble Championships. On the occasion below, the event was held at the South Cumberland Ballpark, c. 1930.

Half of a stereograph taken c. 1890, the view at right looks down from Will's Mountain to the Cumberland Narrows through which the National Road, old U.S. Route 40, travels.

Will's Creek, far right, wends its way through the Narrows, with railroad tracks on both sides of the valley. In the past, one set belonged to the Baltimore & Ohio Railroad, the other to the Western Maryland Railway.

Over the years, Cumberland has endured more flood damage than any other city in Maryland. Water levels of nearly thirty feet have been recorded. The great flood of 1924, pictured below, caused irreparable damage to the Chesapeake & Ohio Canal, and it was never again used for commercial transport.

Mount Savage at one time was a center for rail-roading, brickmaking, and mining both iron and coal.

These two Mount Savage women seem to have had second thoughts about having their portrait made, though the photographer apparently didn't notice.

The Clarysville Inn, above, was built in 1807 to accommodate travelers on the National Road. During the Civil War it was transformed into a Union hospital.

This group of Mount Savage blacksmiths chose to exhibit not only their muscles but also the tools of their trade when this picture was taken.

307

Little did Meshach Frost realize when he opened a tavern in 1812 on a spot he called Mount Pleasant that it would develop into bustling Frostburg, right. In 1901 the streetcar arrived, linking the city with Cumberland and other nearby communities.

The olfactory nerves were always the first to register that the westward traveler was approaching Luke, home of West Virginia Pulp and Paper Company, below.

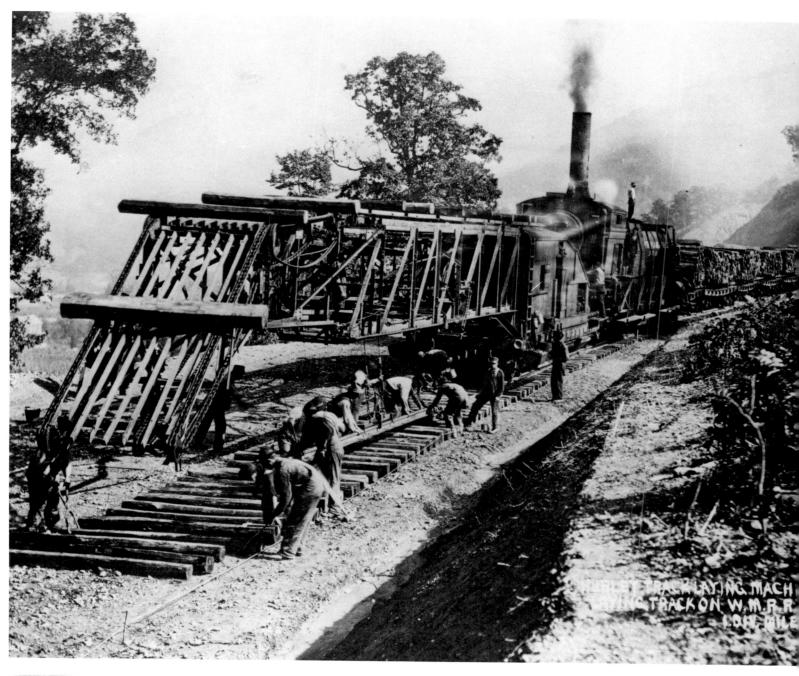

Improving and expanding rail lines must have seemed a never-ending task. On September 23, 1911, crews for the Western Maryland Railway worked to keep pace with a Hurley track-laying machine.

Evidently it was lunchtime when the photographer arrived at Eckhart Mines near Frostburg. The miners, some no more than children, posed with their gear and lunch pails.

Perhaps the most extraordinary feature of this village in Garrett County is its unusual name. In 1774 William Deakins accidentally surveyed the same piece of land which Brooks Beall had marked the day before. Thus when a town was established on the same site about 1800, the name Accident seemed appropriate.

If photographer Leo J. Beachy made both of these photographs of Accident on the same day, it's no wonder that the street scene was deserted: everyone in town was attending the festivities at the Accident school, below.

The store above serviced the small community of McHenry, located at the northernmost tip of Deep Creek Lake, the largest body of fresh water in the state. The lake was constructed from 1923 to 1925 as part of a hydroelectric project. Leo Beachy's photograph of McHenry was probably made several years before.

When the Emory family gave a picnic in Bittinger, left, everyone was invited, including Leo Beachy who recorded the event with his camera.

Schools in Garrett County, as in many rural areas, were often one-room buildings where children of various ages were instructed by one teacher. It had already snowed by November 16 when Mr. King and his pupils stepped outside the McHenry schoolhouse to have their picture made, right.

Living in log cabins and working at spinning wheels remained a way of life for many well into the twentieth century.

The harsh winters of Garrett County probably explain why this home had few windows. The case on the tree stump in the foreground may have held the photographer's equipment.

Arithmetic and spelling lessons evidently were interrupted when this picture was taken.

Meshach Browning, author of Forty-four Years of the Life of a Hunter, *once lived in the cabin, far left, at Sang Run. By his own count, Browning killed 1,800 to 2,000 deer, at least 300 bears, about 50 panthers and catamounts, and scores of wolves and wildcats. He is said to have boxed a bear and wrestled with a full-grown buck.*

If Browning's accounts were accurate, he must have seriously depleted the bear population of the area. When these hunters bagged a black bear (tied to the front of the car) in 1931, it was the first killed near Sang Run in forty years. Their first stop, obviously, was Bell's photographic studio—to have their prize recorded.

The village of Jennings no longer exists, but it was once home of the Maryland Smokeless Coal Company, below.

315

Deer Park

from *The Book of the Royal Blue*, May 1900

Of American mountain resorts, Deer Park, Maryland, is perhaps the most ideal resort that can be found. On the top of the Alleghenies, at an elevation of 3,000 feet above the level of the sea, is a broad plateau, nine miles in width; a beautiful plain of luxuriant vegetation high up in the air. It is on this plateau the splendid hotels of Deer Park and the cottages in connection therewith are built. During the hottest summer months, the air which is always in motion, is simply delightful and the temperature is naturally much lower than it is in the valley on either side of the great mountain range.

This plateau is known as the "Glades" and the Deer Park hotels and their family of cottages occupy a lovely tract of land of five hundred acres in its midst. The original forests are still maintained, much to the credit of the resort, and excellent roadways have been built across the mountains to afford good drive-ways and bicycling.

The splendid hotel buildings, with large airy rooms and immense verandas, are on the top of a knoll, with a beautiful lawn sloping gently to the railway station, not three hundred yards away. The

Roaming "the Glades" at Deer Park c. 1905, these men were perhaps searching for the cottages that an advertising pamphlet described as "scattered promiscuously through the forest, connected by foot paths and drives."

buildings are divided into three parts, known as the Main Building, the East and West Annexes. They are built on the very edge of forest facing the plain, through which the Baltimore & Ohio Railroad wends its way. The ten or twelve cottages belonging to the hotel, which are taken every summer by families, lie about six hundred yards to the east of the building and are connected with well laid out pathways and drives. Architecturally, the whole scene is most

pleasing to the eye and the Park presents the appearance of a small modern city.

The hotel is supplied with every conceivable modern appliance for the convenience of its guests; in fact, there is nothing omitted to please the tastes of the most fastidious person. It is provided with its own gas, electric plants and water system. The sewerage and sanitary arrangement are the best that modern engineering could conceive. Connected with the hotel are two large swimming pools, one for the exclusive use of ladies and children and the other for gentlemen; the temperature of the water being regulated by a complete system of heating. Turkish and Russian baths are also connected with the swimming pools. In a supplementary amusement building or Casino are the billiard and pool tables and bowling alley.

In many of our large hotels and clubs and on the dining cars of several railroads will be found this significant sentence: ''Deer Park Spring Water Used On This Table.'' The spring which furnishes this famous water is known as ''Boiling Spring'' and issues from the rocky heart of the mountain, about a mile and a half from the hotel buildings. It has a daily flow of 150,000 gallons of purest crystal clear water and supplies all of the water used at the hotel and adjacent buildings. Aside from this, a regular business is carried on bottling this water and sending it to many of the Eastern cities. The Spring is encased in a wire-house, securely roofed and locked to absolutely prevent all impurities falling therein.

The great overflow of water, it will be interesting to know, forms the headwaters of the Youghiogheny River, which flows in a narrow, but very deep cut through the plain. This river, or as it is more generally known, the ''Little Yough,'' flows westward through Moun-

Mountain Lake Park, above, was the home of the Mountain Chautauqua, established in 1881. More than two hundred cottages and houses as well as four first-class hotels accommodated visitors to the resort, which occupied about eight hundred acres adjacent to Deer Park. The Chautauquas were nondenominational educational programs with distinctly Christian overtones. Lectures, recitals, and the like were given by prominent artists and ministers each summer. In 1900 an auditorium with a seating capacity of four thousand persons was constructed.

tain Lake Park and Oakland, then turns directly northward, flowing down the western side of the mountain range toward Pittsburgh.

Deer Park has always been a popular resort for the three summer months during which it is opened—from the middle of June to the middle of September. It is the easiest resort to reach in the United States, as one may take a Pullman car in Chicago, St. Louis, Louisville, Cincinnati, Toledo, Columbus, Wheeling, Pittsburg, Washington, Baltimore, Philadelphia or New York, without change of cars, and this is a special inducement to those who wish to avoid the annoyance of the hot summer travel.

The season of 1900 promises to eclipse all other seasons, as the cottages have been engaged for the summer and the hotel has booked a larger percentage of guests so early in the season than at any other period.

Located on the B & O Railroad near Oakland, Deer Park was for many years a famous and favorite resort for vacationers from New York, Chicago, St. Louis, Baltimore, and Washington, D.C. The building at left was the east annex of the Deer Park Hotel.

317

Oakland is the largest town in rural Garrett County, the seat of government, and the business center for the surrounding farming country. The *Garrett* Journal *office was well stocked with office and school supplies.*

On Memorial Day 1903, the Knights of St. John donned their uniforms and joined the Knights of Pythias, and a stray dog, for a group portrait on Alder Street, above.

Several years later members of the Ku Klux Klan disguised themselves in a very different sort of uniform for their parade through Oakland.

Martin's Livery Stables in Oakland, left, provided transportation for visitors to Garrett County's numerous resorts.

Close inspection of the photograph below reveals that the focus of the crowd's attention was a sewing machine that apparently was given away as part of a promotion gimmick.

FOLLOWING PAGES:
It was a quiet day on the National Road when two families paused for Leo Beachy's camera on Negro Mountain, the highest point on the road in Maryland. When Colonel Thomas Cresap and his troops fought a skirmish with a band of Indians on this spot during the French and Indian War, a giant black soldier named Nemesis was killed and buried here, and the mountain was dedicated to his memory.

The Maryland and West Virginia Boundary Commission, right, paused during their surveying efforts to have an informal portrait taken, complete with the camp cook.

The landmark bridge across the Casselman River at Grantsville was built in 1816. Many doubted at the time whether the structure would stand when its supporting framework was removed. By 1900 the bridge was in severe disrepair. Photographer Leo J. Beachy championed its restoration and took numerous pictures and wrote articles to call attention to the situation. After the restoration was completed, Beachy made the classic picture–post-card view below and titled it "The Ocean-to-Ocean Speedway."

THE OCEAN TO OCEAN SPEEDWAY GRANTSVILLE, MD.

Leo J. Beachy began taking photographs of his native Grantsville in 1901 after a brief career as a school teacher. From adolescence on he was severely handicapped by multiple sclerosis, so much so that his sister had to carry him about on her back. She also transported his cumbersome photographic equipment (all of his exposures were made on glass plates).

Knowing this, one finds Beachy's photographs of everyday life in and around Grantsville—like picnics by the river in summer or harvesting ice in winter—all the more remarkable for their apparent spontaneity. (For a fuller appreciation of Beachy's art, see the Introduction.) It is apparent that Beachy was well known and trusted by his friends and neighbors. When the photographer died in 1927 at the age of fifty-three, a tribute appeared in the local newspaper which recognized that ''many years from hence we may still hear the name of Leo J. Beachy extolled as a benefactor to his community as well as to the world at large.''

323

Leo Beachy was also a talented writer. He penned articles and poetry for the local Mennonite church newspaper. At right, members of the congregation gathered for a bountiful picnic.

The area around New Germany, a few miles from Grantsville, was developed into a state park with excellent fishing and swimming facilities and cabins for vacationers. Maryland's first ski slope opened here in the winter of 1940–41.

Logging was a big industry throughout Western Maryland. This camp at Jennings was obviously a productive one where both men and horses earned their keep at the time Leo Beachy made his photograph, c. 1915. By 1940 Jennings was a ghost town.

The touring car provided a popular means for seeing the countryside during the first quarter of this century. Most accommodated five or six adults comfortably; some of the early models achieved astounding speeds of up to twenty miles an hour.

Maple syrup is a thriving industry in the Grantsville area. Sap is collected from sugar maple trees and slowly simmered to boil off excess water. The resulting syrup and sugar are frequently bought by northern dealers and marketed under a Vermont label. The maple sugar camp above was operated by the Engles family near Grantsville.

The country store often doubled as the local post office; it was a social center as well as a source of basic supplies for farmers.

FOLLOWING PAGES:
Leo Beachy's bittersweet caption for his portrait of a friend patiently sitting by the Casselman River, American flag in hand, was "Love Waiteth For Your Return, My Soldier Boy."

Netting was often used to keep flies from bothering horses as they pulled buggies and carriages. Grantsville, with its Amish and Mennonite communities, is among the few places in Maryland where horse-drawn vehicles are still seen on a daily basis.

One can only hope that the marriage of Ethel Warnick and Warren Dill fared better than the wilting fern fronds used to decorate the ceremony held at the bride's home in Grantsville.

327

Select Bibliography

Anderson, Elizabeth B. *Annapolis: A Walk Through History.* Centreville, Md.: Tidewater Publishers, 1984.

Baker, Russell. *Growing Up.* New York: Congdon & Weed, 1982.

Blair, Carvel Hall, and Willits Dyer Ansel. *Chesapeake Bay Notes & Sketches.* Cambridge, Md.: Tidewater Publishers, 1970.

Corddry, George H. *Wicomico County History.* Salisbury, Md.: Peninsula Press, 1981.

Dorchester County: A Pictorial History. Cambridge, Md.: Western Publishing Co., 1977.

Footner, Hulbert. *Maryland Main and the Eastern Shore.* New York: D. Appleton-Century Co., 1942.

Gannett, Henry. *Maryland and Delaware: A Gazetteer.* 1904. Reprint. Baltimore: Genealogical Publishing Co., 1979.

Greene, Suzanne Ellery. *Baltimore: An Illustrated History.* Woodland Hills, Calif.: Windsor Publications, 1980.

Hahn, Thomas F. *Chesapeake and Ohio Canal Old Picture Album.* Shepherdstown, W. Va.: The American Canal & Transportation Center, 1976.

Hawthorne, Hildegarde. *Rambles in Old College Towns.* New York: Dodd, Mead & Co., 1917.

Kelly, Jacques. *Maryland: A Pictorial History, the First 350 Years.* Norfolk, Va.: The Donning Company, 1983.

Krech, Shepard, III. *Praise the Bridge That Carries You Over: The Life of Joseph L. Sutton.* Cambridge, Mass.: Schenkman Publishing Co., 1981.

Martin, Oliver. *The Chesapeake and Potomac Country.* The Chesapeake and Potomac Telephone Co., 1928.

Maryland State Planning Commission and Department of Geology, Mines and Water Resources. *Gazetteer of Maryland.* Baltimore: Maryland State Planning Commission, 1941.

McCoy, A. R. *Stray Thoughts: A Collection of Essays, Incidents and Stories.* Baltimore: Charles Harvey & Co., 1876.

McMurry, Donald L. *Coxey's Army: A Study of the Industrial Movement of 1894.* Seattle: University of Washington Press, 1929.

Olson, Sherry H. *Baltimore: The Building of an American City.* The Johns Hopkins University Press, 1980.

Papenfuse, Edward C., Gregory A. Stiverson, Susan A. Collins, and Lois Green Carr, eds. *Maryland: A New Guide to the Old Line State.* Baltimore: The Johns Hopkins University Press, 1976.

Schlotterbeck, Judith A. *The Pen Mar Story.* Funkstown, Md.: Tri-State Printing, 1977.

Schwartz, Lee G., Albert L. Feldstein, and Joan H. Baldwin. *A Pictorial History of Allegany County.* Norfolk, Va.: The Donning Co., 1980.

Stapp, William F., and Marjorie L. Share. *Picture It!* Washington, D. C.: Smithsonian Institution Traveling Exhibition Service, 1981.

The Book of the Royal Blue. 12 vols. Baltimore: The Baltimore & Ohio Railroad, 1898–1910.

The Telephone in Maryland. Baltimore: The Chesapeake and Potomac Telephone Co. of Maryland, 1974.

Tilghman, Tench Francis. *The Early History of St. John's College in Annapolis.* Annapolis, Md.: St. John's College Press, 1984.

Toomey, Daniel Carroll. *The Civil War in Maryland.* Baltimore: Toomey Press, 1983.

Warren, Mame, and Marion E. Warren. *Everybody Works But John Paul Jones: A Portrait of the U. S. Naval Academy 1845–1915.* Annapolis, Md.: Naval Institute Press, 1981.

Warren, Marion E., and Mame Warren. *Baltimore: When She Was What She Used to Be, 1850–1930.* Baltimore: The Johns Hopkins University Press, 1983.

Warren, Marion E., and Mame Warren. *The Train's Done Been and Gone: An Annapolis Portrait 1859–1910.* Boston: David R. Godine, 1976.

White, Clarence Marbury, Sr., and Evangeline Kaiser White. *The Years Between: A Chronicle of Annapolis, Maryland 1800–1900, and Memoirs.* New York: Exposition Press, 1957.

Williams, Ames W. *Otto Mears Goes East: The Chesapeake Beach Railway.* Prince Frederick, Md.: Calvert County Historical Society, 1975.

Writers' Program of the Work Projects Administration in the State of Maryland. *Maryland: A Guide to the Old Line State.* New York: Oxford University Press, 1940.

Photograph Credits

Roman and arabic numerals refer to page numbers.

a=above   al=above left   ar=above right   b=below   bl=below left   br=below right   c=center

SOURCES

ALLEGANY COUNTY HISTORICAL SOCIETY 292b, 294a, 296–97, 303a, 304b, 307b, 309b

BALTIMORE COUNTY PUBLIC LIBRARY, CATONSVILLE BRANCH 92a, 96b, 97a, 97c, 97b

BALTIMORE COUNTY PUBLIC LIBRARY, REISTERSTOWN BRANCH 93b, 94a, 94c, 94b, 95a, 95b

BALTIMORE COUNTY PUBLIC LIBRARY, TOWSON BRANCH 90a, 90c, 90b, 91a, 91b

BALTIMORE GAS & ELECTRIC COMPANY 85b, 108b, 123a, 123c, 123bl, 123br, 130, 134–35, 137a, 137c, 137b, 142b, 151a, 151b, 155b, 158a, 158b, 160–61

BALTIMORE MUSEUM OF INDUSTRY 143b, 156b, 157b

POLLY BARBER 214a, 216–17

DOUG BAST viii–ix, xviii, 270–71, 272a, 272b, 273a, 273c, 280b

ENALEE BOUNDS 109b

SPECIAL COLLECTIONS, THURGOOD MARSHALL LIBRARY, BOWIE STATE COLLEGE 230b, 231a, 231b

MAXINE BEACHY BROADWATER xix, xxii, xxiv, 310a, 310b, 311a, 311b, 313a, 313b, 314, 320–21, 322b, 323a, 323b, 324a, 324b, 325a, 325b, 326a, 327a, 327b, 328–29

CALIFORNIA MUSEUM OF PHOTOGRAPHY AT THE UNIVERSITY OF CALIFORNIA AT RIVERSIDE 122a, 181, 184b

CARROLL COUNTY HISTORICAL SOCIETY 100a, 100b, 101a, 101b, 102, 103a, 103b, 104b, 105a, 105b, 106b, 107c

CHARLES COUNTY EXTENSION OFFICE 215c, 222a, 222b

CHESAPEAKE & OHIO CANAL MUSEUM 116–17

CHESAPEAKE & POTOMAC TELEPHONE COMPANY 150b, 157a, 167

CHESAPEAKE BEACH RAILWAY MUSEUM 204a, 204b, 205a, 205c, 205b, 206b, 207c, 207b, 208a, 208bl, 208br, 209

LAURANCE G. CLAGGETT 20a, 27a, 29, 34b, 39b, 40a, 40c, 46a, 47b, 49a, 52b, 87c, 88–89, 222c, 261a, 306a

COLUMBIA HISTORICAL SOCIETY 228a, 228b

CITY OF CUMBERLAND, HERMAN AND STACIA MILLER COLLECTION xx, xxiii, 286, 287b, 290a, 292a, 293b, 294b, 295a, 295c, 295b, 296a, 296b, 297a, 297b, 298a, 298b, 299a, 299c, 299b, 300a, 301a, 301b, 302a, 302c, 302bl, 302br, 303b, 304a, 307a, 308a, 312b

HILDA CUSHWA 108a, 261b

DEPARTMENT OF NATURAL RESOURCES 273b

DORCHESTER COUNTY HEALTH DEPARTMENT 54

TISH DRYDEN 10c, 10b

DUNN CONSTRUCTION COMPANY 182–83

ROBERT ENNIS 237b

ENOCH PRATT FREE LIBRARY vi–vii, 24c, 139, 162b, 172c, 203, 220–21, 283c, 289b

KATHERINE ETCHISON 13a

MR. AND MRS. JACK FRANCIS 174b, 176b

FREDERICK COUNTY HISTORICAL SOCIETY 246b, 247b, 248a, 248b, 251, 252a, 252b, 253, 254, 255a, 255b, 257c, 257b, 258a, 258c, 258b, 259a, 259b, 262b, 263b

GARRETT COUNTY HISTORICAL SOCIETY 312a, 315a, 318a, 318c, 318b, 319a, 319b, 322a, 326b

NORMA GREEN, 51a

CARROLL GREENE, JR. 172a, 173a, 173b

JAN GREISMAN 113a, 113b

ELOUISE HARDING 53a, 53c, 64, 65a, 65b, 66a, 66b, 67, 87b, 109c, 133a, 136a, 150a, 154a, 162a, 162c, 206a, 207a

HARFORD COUNTY HISTORICAL SOCIETY 80a, 80b, 81a, 81c, 81b, 83c, 84a, 84b, 85c

LOIS HARRISON 9c

RAYMOND HICKS 93a, 104a, 266b, 267a, 267c, 267b, 268a, 269, 290b, 300b, 305, 309a, 315b

HISTORICAL SOCIETY OF CECIL COUNTY 70a, 70b, 71a, 71b, 73a, 73b, 74a, 74c, 74b, 75b, 76a, 76b, 77a, 77c, 77b

HISTORICAL SOCIETY OF MONTGOMERY COUNTY 114a, 114c, 114b, 115a, 115c, 115b

HISTORICAL SOCIETY OF TALBOT COUNTY 4b, 14a, 30a, 32–33, 35a, 40b, 41a, 41b, 42b, 43a, 43b, 51b

HISTORY DIVISION OF THE MARYLAND–NATIONAL CAPITAL PARK AND PLANNING COMMISSION 229b, 233b, 235b, 236a

WILLIAM HOLLIFIELD 69a, 72a, 72b, 83a, 83b, 92c, 109a, 122b, 136b, 237c, 257a, 308b, 317a

HOWARD COUNTY HISTORICAL SOCIETY 110, 111a, 111b

HARRY JONES 222b

MORLEY AND JUDY JULL 22, 23a, 24b, 25b, 26a, 26b, 28, 31b

KENNETH KAUMEYER 164

MILDRED KEMP 38

LIBRARY OF CONGRESS xvi, 2, 20b, 27b, 37b, 55, 58, 59, 118a, 118b, 119b, 156a, 182b, 189a, 193a, 232b, 266a, 316, 317b

JOSIE LINES 210b, 211a

MICHAEL LUBY 9b, 10a, 12a, 12b, 13c, 34c, 35b, 36a, 36b, 37a, 39a, 42a, 42c, 44a, 45a, 45c, 45b, 47a, 48a, 48b, 60a, 69b, 75a, 120a, 174a

ROBERT SADLER MCCENEY 52a, 53b, 169a, 170a, 170b, 214b, 232a, 238a, 238c, 238b, 239a, 239b

MARYLAND HALL OF RECORDS ii–iii, 14b, 15a, 57b, 61a, 98–99, 171a, 175al, 175b, 177c, 183b, 184a, 187, 192b, 193c, 194–95, 196a, 196c, 196b, 197a, 197b, 198, 200b, 201b, 200–201, 202c, 202b, 212b

MARYLAND HISTORICAL SOCIETY 25a, 87a, 106a, 112a, 119c, 121, 124b, 132a, 138, 236b, 279b, 293a

VIRGINIA MEREDITH 180a

ROBERT G. MERRICK 78

LEROY MERRIKEW 131b

A. N. MILLER 250a

NATIONAL ARCHIVES 224a, 224b, 225

OCEAN CITY LIFE–SAVING STATION MUSEUM 4a, 5a, 5b, 6–7, 8a, 21b

PEALE MUSEUM 126, 127, 128c, 128b, 129a, 129b, 132c, 140a, 140b, 141, 146

EBE POPE 8b, 21a

FRANCES G. POTTER 23b

PRINCE GEORGE'S COUNTY HISTORICAL SOCIETY 229a, 234–35, 237a

PAUL RANDALL 226, 227a, 227c, 227b

MRS. WILLIAM ROWE 92b

ST. MARY'S CHURCH ARCHIVE, ANNAPOLIS 175ar

ST. MARY'S CITY COMMISSION 212a, 213, 215a, 215b, 218a, 218b, 219, 220b

MARY SEMEY SCHMIDT 49b

FRANKLIN SHAW iv–v, 107a, 107b, 199, 242a, 242b, 243a, 243b, 244–45, 249, 250b, 260, 262a

VIRGINIA TURNER SOMERVILLE 210a

SOUTH RIVER CLUB 202a

STEAMSHIP HISTORICAL SOCIETY 163a

SUSQUEHANNA MUSEUM OF HAVRE DE GRACE 82a, 82b

PETER TASI 149a

DAN TOOMEY 112b, 120b, 185b

SPECIAL COLLECTIONS, U. S. NAVAL ACADEMY, NIMITZ LIBRARY 177a, 190, 191b

EDWARD L. BAFFORD PHOTOGRAPHY COLLECTION, UNIVERSITY OF MARYLAND, BALTIMORE COUNTY 88a, 89a, 144a, 144b, 145a, 145c, 145b

SPECIAL COLLECTIONS, UNIVERSITY OF MARYLAND, COLLEGE PARK LIBRARIES 15b, 56, 57a, 143a, 154b, 155a, 159, 169b, 171b, 177b, 223a, 233a, 233c, 247a

M. E. WARREN PHOTOGRAPHY 34a, 85a, 86a, 96a, 147al, 147ar, 147b, 148b, 172b, 176a, 178–79, 180b, 185a, 186, 188, 191c, 230a, 274, 277a, 277b, 278b

WASHINGTON COUNTY FREE LIBRARY 240, 280a, 281a, 284–85, 287a, 289a, 291a

WASHINGTON COUNTY HISTORICAL SOCIETY i, 119a, 166, 246a, 256, 263a, 268b, 278a, 281b, 282a, 282b, 283a, 283b, 288a, 288b, 291b

WASHINGTON NAVY YARD 189b, 191a, 192a, 193b

The Johns Hopkins University Press

MARYLAND TIME EXPOSURES

This book was composed in Palatino by BG Composition, Inc., Baltimore, Maryland, from a design by Gerard A. Valerio.

It was printed on 80-lb. Warren's Lustro Offset Enamel by the Collins Lithographing and Printing Company, Baltimore, Maryland, and bound in Holliston Record Buckram by the Optic Bindery, Baltimore, Maryland.